T0123435

MY EVERLASTING EDUCATION AT SAINT FINBARR'S COLLEGE
ACADEMICS, DISCIPLINE, AND SPORTS

DEJI BADIRU

MY EVERLASTING EDUCATION AT SAINT FINBARR'S COLLEGE: ACADEMICS, DISCIPLINE, AND SPORTS

iUniverse books may be ordered through booksellers or by contacting:

iUniverse
1663 Liberty Drive
Bloomington, IN 47403
www.iuniverse.com
1-800-Authors (1-800-288-4677)

ISBN: 978-1-5320-9863-5 (sc)
ISBN: 978-1-5320-9864-2 (e)

Library of Congress Control Number: 2020909354

Print information available on the last page.

iUniverse rev. date: 05/22/2020

Adedeji Badiru writes as the primary author for ABICS Publications (www.abicspublications.com), A Division of AB International Consulting Services, dedicated to publishing books for home, work, and leisure.

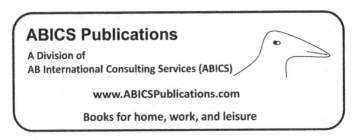

ABICS Publications
A Division of
AB International Consulting Services (ABICS)

www.ABICSPublications.com

Books for home, work, and leisure

Books in the ABICS Publications book series, published by iUniverse, Inc., on recreational, educational, motivational, and personal development books, include the titles below:

My Everlasting Education at Saint Finbarr's College: Academics, Discipline, and Sports

Secret of the 25th Hour in the Day: Getting More Done Each Day

Kitchen Project Management: The Art and Science of an Organized Kitchen

Wives of the Same School: Tributes and Straight Talk

The Rooster and the Hen: Story of Love at Last Look

The Story of Saint Finbarr's College: Contributions to Education and Sports Development in Nigeria

Physics of Soccer II: Science and Strategies for a Better Game

Kitchen Dynamics: The rice way

Consumer Economics: The value of dollars and sense for money management

Youth Soccer Training Slides: A Math and Science Approach

My Little Blue Book of Project Management

8 by 3 Paradigm for Time Management

Badiru's Equation of Student Success: Intelligence, Common Sense, and Self-discipline

Isi Cookbook: Collection of Easy Nigerian Recipes

Blessings of a Father: Education contributions of Father Slattery at Saint Finbarr's College

Physics in the Nigerian Kitchen: The Science, the Art, and the Recipes

The Physics of Soccer: Using Math and Science to Improve Your Game

Getting things done through project management

Dedication

Dedicated to all my educational mentors of the past, present, and future. The good deeds of many of these mentors have shaped the way I have committed myself over the years to support and advance the educational pursuits of others. Some names that should be mentioned, in addition to my own family members, are Sid and Pat Gilbreath, Carroll Viera (nee Carroll Miller), late Gary Whitehouse, Ravi Ravindran, and George Igbuan (Baba Monday).

Contents

Acknowledgments

I thank all my fellow Saint Finbarr's College conquerors for their friendship and fellowship over the years. There are too many to name in a brief acknowledgment statement. However, my special expression of gratitude goes to Derek Oladokun, who joyfully took my personal photo that is used in the front cover of this book. We all appreciate his altruistic leveraging of his photography skills and interest for the benefit of Saint Finbarr's programs and events. At the Nigerian end of the activities of the "Old Boys" of Saint Finbarr's College, I am delighted to recognize the long-standing and consistent leadership of Segun Ajanlekoko, Yinka Bashorun, and Benedict Ikwenobe. These gentlemen never fail to answer the call of Finbarr's. They have served the school and the alumni association in various forms at various active levels for multiple decades. That is a true mark of demonstrating Fidelitas. They are all much appreciated! At the Ireland end of the spectrum, my distinct thanks go to Mr. Joe Slattery, Father Slattery's nephew in Fermoy, Ireland, who has kept vigil over the continuing connectivity of Finbarr's to the Slattery Family of Ireland. He and his wife, Catherine, continue to be favorite friends and fans of Finbarr's.

Introduction to Saint Finbarr's College

Education is the bastion of national advancement and workforce development. If we want a sustainable economic and intellectual development of a nation, we must invest in education. Education should be an entitlement of every citizen of every nation. Unfortunately, education is often brushed aside, poorly funded, or crosshatched in many political wrangling in many nations. The premise of my writing this book is not only to sing the praises of Saint Finbarr's College, but also to illuminate the value of education across the spectrum of human endeavors. Even in the pursuit of national defense, which often gets a hefty budget, I opine that education could be a powerful weapon of national defense. Education is multidimensional in effect and can solve a variety of national problems.

Education is a universal asset that opens the world up to all those fortunate enough to receive it at an opportune time in life. I was fortunate to have received an everlasting educational foundation at Saint Finbarr's College (SFC), Lagos, Nigeria. In many instances, the school is affectionately referred to simply as "Finbarr's."

The declaration by Nelson Mandela, the late South African elder statesman, taught us that:

"Education is the most powerful weapon
you can use to change the world."

He made this statement in the context of social and economic advancement of not only his people, but also for the entire world. The solid education provided by Saint Finbarr's College has continued to change the world, through worldwide accomplishments of the school's graduates. In both small and large ways, Ex-Finbarrians spread the ideals of the school through personal, professional, and spiritual platforms. This perpetuation of the school's educational contributions is my motivation for writing this book. The exceptional professional footprints of Finbarr's graduates span all sorts of career pursuits, including the following:

Academics
Architecture
Banking
Business
Civil service
Clergy
Coaching
Construction
Consulting
Culinary arts
Design
Economics
Education administration
Engineering
Entrepreneur
Evangelist
Finance
Fine Arts
Government
Law enforcement
Legal profession
Manufacturing
Mathematics
Medicine
Military

Ministering
Motivational speaking
Photography
Politics
Priesthood
Restauranteur
Science
Social science
Sports
Technology
Trading

The school and its contributions are celebrated on the pages of what lies ahead of readers.

What is gained, learned, and earned through education stays with a person throughout his or her lifetime. This led to the choice of this book's title of "My Everlasting Education at Saint Finbarr's College." May the message stick in the minds of all readers.

This book is the fourth in my series of books celebrating the glory of Saint Finbarr's College and its founder, late Reverend Denis Joseph Slattery. If you have read the previous books, you might notice similarities in the contends and stories presented. This is by design. Oftentimes, duplications and repeats are essential for spreading the good word far and wide so that notable achievements are not forgotten. The Chinese Philosopher, Confucius, enjoined us with the following statement:

"Tell me and I forget;
Show me and I remember;
Involve me and I understand."

I attended Saint Finbarr's College from January 1968 through December 1972 and my life has continued to be enriched by that unique experience.

My purpose in this book is to tell, show, and involve readers so that we can all understand how the good examples from Saint Finbarr's College and Father Slattery can be fully understood for the purpose of replicating them elsewhere and everywhere. The previous books that provide the foundation for this current book are listed below.

1. *Blessings of a Father: A Tribute to the Life and Work of Reverend Father Denis Joseph Slattery* (printed in 2005 both in Nigeria and USA).

2. **Blessings of a Father: Education contributions of Father Slattery at Saint Finbarr's** College (published in 2013)

3. **The Story of Saint Finbarr's College: Father Slattery's Contributions to Education and Sports in Nigeria** (published in 2018)

The foci of the first three books had been either the school itself or Father Slattery himself (Badiru (2005, 2013, 2018). This current book focuses on "education" as the main character or "star" of the narrations on the pages therein contained. The worldwide power of education is conveyed in the words of Malala Yousafzai, the Pakistani girl, whom the Taliban attempted to kill with a bullet because of her activism for female education in 2012. She survived. She later said:

> **"Extremists have shown what frightens**
> **them most: A Girl with a Book."**

Malala later became the youngest Nobel Laureate for her commitment to mobilizing education of women.

In effect, education has many lifelong benefits. The one that is most readily noticed is the ability to read and write, in the sense that an educated person is said to be literate. Actually, beyond literacy, education has more subtle benefits, such as critical thinking, empathy, social connectivity, sense of responsibility, global awareness, collaborative fellowship, and so on. Education at Saint Finbarr's College instilled many desirable characteristics in the students. What I am today, professionally and personally, is the product of the educational and discipline foundations that I acquired at Saint Finbarr's College. For this, I remain eternally grateful.

Even though Finbarr's is a Catholic school, non-denominational education is the product of Saint Finbarr's College, at least at the time that I went through the school. Whichever focus is chosen for writing a book about Saint Finbarr's College, the stories of the school and the Father are intertwined. I cannot write about one without touching on the aspects of the other. The three main attributes that characterize Saint Finbarr's College are:

1. **Academics**
2. **Discipline**
3. **Sports (most notably, soccer)**

We adore these three attributes deeply. So proud are the Boys of Finbarr's (or Finbarrians), as cherish to be called, that we seek all kinds of opportunities to celebrate the school. Two examples shown in Figure 1 are the school ring and lapel pin. The cover of this book is adorned with the author wearing the famous blazer of Saint Finbarr's College. The nickname for Saint Finbarr's College is The Conquerors. You will see this name in our sports songs, insignias, and documents.

Figure 1. Saint Finbarr's College School Ring and Lapel Pin

The organization of this book centers around the three unique attributes of Saint Finbarr's College: Academics, Discipline, and Sports). They are addressed sequentially in the chapters that follow.

My first book on Saint Finbarr's College was launched publicly with national fanfare in Lagos, Nigeria on July 5, 2005. The invitation card for the event is shown in Figure 2. All the proceeds from the book launch were donated to the school. In addition, over 700 additional copies were donated to the school for subsequent fundraising programs. The school administration acknowledged the book donation in a January 14, 2006 conversation, which I recall as follows:

Congratulations on the 50th anniversary of your Alma Mater, may we continue to enjoy the blessings and graces of the Founder and God. Thanks a lot for your contributions and encouragement to me in particular, may God grant us our desires for the school. As part of the school's programme for the anniversary, we intend to relaunch your book, 'THE FATHER'S BLESSINGS'. We still have some copies with us, about seven hundred. I hope we have your permission to do this? If I can recollect, you did say at the launching that the proceeds from the launchings should go to the school. I am just reminding you of this for clarity sake so that there wouldn't be any misgivings between the school and the Alumni. We wouldn't know how to thank you enough. May God give you the necessary blessings.

In that conversation, I reassured the school with my pledge, recalled as the following:

Yes, you have my permission to re-launch the book as a part of our ongoing revitalization programmes for Saint Finbarr's College. Yes, indeed, all proceeds from the book should go to the school as a part of the contribution from the USA Branch of SFCOBA. It will be appreciated if SFCOBA can be apprised of the specific projects accomplished with the money raised from the book. If you publicize the re-launching of the book very well, I am sure we can raise a lot of money. When you have the information about the re-launching ready, please send me a copy so that I can forward it to my friends who did not have an opportunity to attend the first launching.

Figure 2. Book Launch Invitation Card

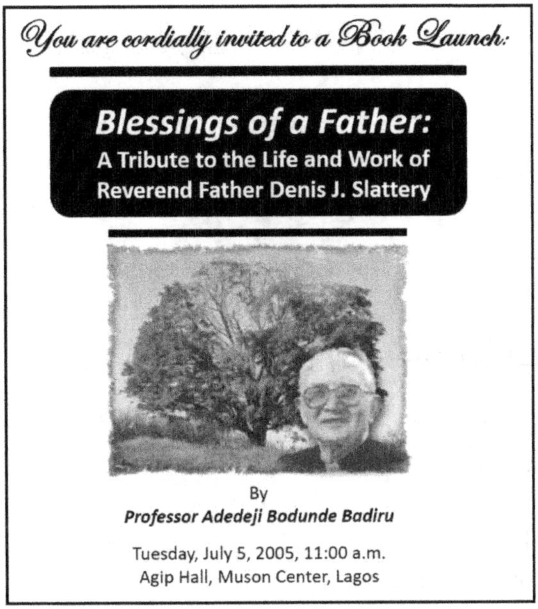

You are cordially invited to a Book Launch:

Blessings of a Father:
A Tribute to the Life and Work of
Reverend Father Denis J. Slattery

By
Professor Adedeji Bodunde Badiru

Tuesday, July 5, 2005, 11:00 a.m.
Agip Hall, Muson Center, Lagos

Songs and Anthems of Saint Finbarr's College

"*Fidelitas*," a Latin word, is the motto (slogan, maxim, dictum, axiom) of Saint Finbarr's College.

It means loyalty, faithfulness, or homage.

The noun fealty is related to fidelity, which is another way of saying loyalty and faithfulness.

Variations of fidelitas include fidelitate, fidelitatem, fidelitates, fidelitatibus, fidelitatis, fidelitatum, and fidelitatis.

The deep meaning of fidelitas is the reason all students and graduates of Saint Finbarr's College harbor extreme pride and loyalty to the ideals of the school. This is embodied and emblazoned in the middle of the emblem (crest, symbol, insignia, logo, badge, motif) of the school shown in Figure 3.

Figure 3. Logo of Saint Finbarr's College

Anthem of Saint Finbarr's College

Saint Finbarr's College, Akoka
My own source of knowledge
I am proud to belong
I am proud to belong
To the citadel of excellence
Fidelitas, Fidelitas
Fi-de-li-tas!

VERSE 1
SAINT FINBARR'S COLLEGE AKOKA
MY OWN ALMA MATA
I'M PROUD TO BELONG
I'M PROUD TO BELONG
TO THE CITADEL OF EXCELLENCE

Chorus:
FIDELITAS...
FIDE-DE-LITAS
FIDELITAS...
FIDE-DE-LITAS
FIDELITAS

VERSE 2
JOY AND HAPPINESS IS OURS
WHENEVER WE REMEMBER YOU

A PLACE EVERYONE x2
IS LOVED AND CARED FOR OOOO

Chorus:
FIDELITAS…
FIDE-DE-LITAS
FIDELITAS…
FIDE-DE-LITAS
FIDELITAS

Warm Up for Finbarr's Songs

Begin Warm Up: (Before start of any song)
Lead: Esobe Zangaruwa
Response: Yeah!
(2ce)

Song 1: GRAND OLD TEAM
We've a grand old team to play for us
Tralalala la la la la. Tra la la la la la
When you read the history, Pam Pam (bang your feet or clap 2ce)
It's enough to cause your heart cheer er er
For we don't care whether we win or lose or draw
The warriors be stared
For we always know there is going to be a match and St Finbarr's College
must be there
Must be there
Finbarr's, Finbarr's
Finbarr's Finbarr's Finbarr's
F I N B A R R ' S - FINBARR'SSSSS!!!!

Song 2: WE PLAY AT TIMES
Lead: We play at times
Response: We play at times
Lead: And race and run
Response: And race and run
Lead: I'll tell you why
Response: I'll tell you why

Lead: For love of game
Response: For love of game
All: Ha ha ha play you Finbarr's play you game
All: Ha ha ha play you Finbarr's play you game for love of game
All: Ha ha ha play you Finbarr's play you game, for fun for love of game
Up School, Up FINBARR'S !!!!!

Song 3: WHEN I WENT TO FINBARR'S

When I went to Finbarr's
What did I see
The Akoka boys were playing with Supreme as their coach
HOLY, singing Hallelujah
Singing Hallelujah, singing Hallelujah, Holy
HOLY, singing Hallelujah
Singing Hallelujah, singing Hallelujah, Holy!!!

Song 4: ZINGA ZINGA BOM BOM

Lead: St Finbarr's
Response: Zinga Zinga Bom Bom, Zinga Zinga
Lead: St Finbarrrrrrrr's
Response: Zinga Zinga Bom Bom, Zinga Zinga
Lead: En goyama goyama
Response: Ya Bom, Ya Bom, Ya bom, Iya Bom.

Song 5: OUR COLOURS

Lead: Our Colours
Response: Blue Yellow Blue
Lead: Our colleagues
Response: Up Finbarr's
All: We shall never, never, never, never lose this match (2ce)
All: We shall never, never, never, never lose this YEAR! Up Finbarr's!

Song 6: OWEGBELUGBO

Lead: Owegbelugbo o
Response: St Finbarr's
Lead: Owegbelugbo
Response: St Finbarr's
Lead: Owegbelugbo o

Response: St Finbarr's
Lead: Owegbelugbo
Response: St Finbarr's
All: Ade o ri wa o
Response: St Finbarr's
All: Owegbelugbo
Response: St Finbarr's
All: Bata ese wa o
Response: St Finbarr's
All: Owegbelugbo o
Lead: Ama nor Igbobi
All: St Finbarr's
Lead: Ama nor St Gregory's
All: St Finbarr's

Song 7: HOLY HOLY (Victory Song)
Holy, holy- Holy, holy! Holy, holy!
St Finbarr's Akoka, another champion
HOLY HOLY (Victory Song)
Holy, holy- Holy, holy! Holy, holy!
St Finbarr's Akoka, another champion
I begi teach them soccer
Oh, oh, oh, oh, oh - oh, oh, oh, oh - oh, oh, oh oh!
I begi show them soccer
Oh, oh, oh, oh, oh - oh, oh, oh, oh - oh, oh, oh oh!

Song 8: WADELE
Lead: Wa de le oh, wa de le oh oh
All: Wa de, wadele oh oh
Lead: Father Slattery eiye wa de le oh oh
All: Wa de, wadele oh oh
Lead: (captain's name, players names) wa de le oh oh
All: Wa de, wadele oh oh
All: Wa de le oh, wa de le oh oh
All: Wa de, wadele oh oh
All: Wa de leeeee wa de le oh (2ce)

Song 9: FINBARR'S BOYS ARE THERE AGAIN
Lead: Finbarr's boys are there again
All: Hallelujah
Lead: To teach them to play soccer
All: Hallelujah
Lead: (Captain's name) is there today
All: Hallelujah

(Charged Version for when the players start scoring goals)
All: Finbarr's Boys have come again oh oh to teach them how to play soccer!!!
Finbarr's Boys oh oh
Have come again
To teach them how to play soccer

Song 10: IF YOU GO TO BRAZIL
Lead: If you go to Brazil and bring Sir Pele
All: Finbarr's are winning today
All: Finbarr's are winning, Finbarr's are winning
All: Finbarr's are winning TODAY!!!

Song 11: **MERRY MERRY ST FINBARR'S**
Merry merry St Finbarr's oh oh
Merry merry St Finbarr's
Ah ah - Ah ah
Merry merry St Finbarr's
Merry merry Father Slattery oh oh
Merry merry Father Slattery
Ah ah - ah ah
Merry merry Father Slattery
(Players names also)

Song 12: **PRAYER HYMN (HOLY QUEEN)**
Holy Queen we bend before Thee
Queen of purity divine
Make us love Thee we implore Thee
Make us truly to be thine

CHORUS
Teach us teach
Teach us teach us Holy Mother
How to conquer every sin
How to love
How to love and help each other
At the prize of life to win

Unto Thee a child was given
Greater than the son of men
Coming down from highest heaven
To create the world again

Chorus - Teach us teach us

Song 13: The proud big boys, they conquered many schools
But when they meet St Finbarr's
We shall throw them to the window
The window, the window the
window, window, window

UP SCHOOL !!!! UP F I N B A R R ' S !!!!!!!!
Assembly Prayers and Hymns of Saint Finbarr's College

Below are my own recollections of some of the popular prayers and hymns for Saint Finbarr's College. The repertoire is probably more expansive nowadays than in my own Finbarr's days.

School Anthem
Saint Finbarr's College
My own alma mater
I am proud to belong
I am proud to belong
To the citadel of excellence
Fidelitas (2ce)
Fidelitas

School Pledge

I pledge to
Saint Finbarr's College as a worthy student
To be loyal to the college Authorities
To respect and cooperate with all staff and Prefects of the college
And obey all rules and regulations of the college
To project the college with pride in good light everywhere and at all times, and
To do all in my power to leave the College better than I met it,
So, help me God.

Assembly Hall Song

(Note: This was a popular assembly-hall song at Saint Finbarr's in the 1970's)

Hail Queen of Heaven (sing):

Hail, Queen of heaven, the ocean star,
Guide of the wanderer here below,
Thrown on life's surge, we claim thy care,
Save us from peril and from woe.

Mother of Christ, O Star of the sea
Pray for the wanderer, pray for me.

In recognition of his multi-faceted contributions and legacy, I composed the ode below to Father Slattery. May his name continue to be immortalized!

My Ode to Reverend Father Slattery

Our father is gone;
Our father is gone;
Our Reverend Father Slattery is gone;
Even though he is no longer with us;
His blessings continue to guide us.
Nature propagates life; mankind finds ways to diminish it.
Throughout his life, Father Slattery pursued ways to rectify the errors of mankind.

An all-embracing School

Although Saint Finbarr's College was a Catholic School (still is), the proprietor, Reverend Denis Joseph Slattery, practiced secular philosophies that embraced all comers, regardless of creed, religion, tribe, tongue, or social status. Moslems attending the school were given a free rein to practice their religion. In fact, Moslems were allowed to leave campus on Fridays to go to Mosques in accordance with the expectation of the Islamic faith. Mischievous kids, who needed a fake excuse to skip campus, were wont to claim the Islamic faith on Fridays.

Origin of Education at Saint Finbarr's College

The story of Saint Finbarr's College is fascinating and inspiring. The story of Saint Finbarr's College is a favorite pastime of all the former and present students of the school, wherever and whenever they gather. Even in times of solitude and safety lockdown, Finbarrians dream, talk, and reflect on Finbarr's ideals. The founder and originator of Saint Finbarr's College was Reverend Father Denis Joseph Slattery, who came to Nigeria in 1941. Having served in a parish at Ilawe-Ekiti, in the Yoruba Inland Town of Ilawe-Ekiti, in the Old Western Region, Father Slattery was posted to Saint Gregory's College, Obalende as a teacher and later became the Games Master. He later became the editor of the Catholic Herald in Mushin. It was during this period that the thought of establishing a unique school occurred to him. His school became the first bilateral school in the country, combining full Grammar (called Basic) with Arts and Technical subjects. In the 1955/56 academic year, with six students, fondly referred to as "the first six of the first six", a new school, but without a name, was born. The "first six of the first six" refers to the first six students in the first six years of Saint Finbarr's College.

The new school had no address and had to be accommodated in the newly-built St. Paul's Catholic Primary School, Abebe Village, Apapa Road, Ebute-Metta, Lagos.

The next task was to look for a site for the new school. Father Slattery, after an eleven-month search, which took him through the then wilderness area of Apapa, now the present location of the National Stadium. Further searches eventually got him to another wilderness area in Akoka, where he met a man who knew Father Slattery, but whom Father Slattery did not know. The friendly disposition of the man made it easy for Father Slattery to acquire a twenty-plot piece of land in the present site of the school. In 1959, the school moved from Apapa Road to its present site in Akoka, and in 1963, the school was officially opened by Dr. Nnamdi Azikiwe, the first President of Nigeria, who was a personal friend of Father Slattery.

In a tactical move, he got a grant from the then British colonial government, with which he set up a ten-classroom block, two technical drawing rooms, a technical block, an administrative block, which also housed the teachers staff room, and a dining-room assembly hall with a well-equipped kitchen. Among the first teachers of the school were the late Chief Albert Bankole, Father Slattery himself, and Mr. F. Ekpeti.

Although a complete and accurate listing of the first set of students is difficult for me to come by at this time, due to the long passage of time, oral accounts indicate that the first set of students, known as Finbarr's First Set (FFS), included the following names:

1. H. A. Williams,
2. G Braimoh
3. A Oriakhi
4. L O Ilesanmi
5. S K Kappo
6. G K Nwokeji
7. A O Odugbesan
8. V O Odiase
9. S Elesha
10. M O Akanji
11. S Browne
12. M Odu
13. F B A Ogundipe
14. S O Enaughe
15. F Ozieh
16. B A Koshoni
17. F A Adedipe
18. J T Oshisanya
19. S Igbonoba
20. J Oladeinde
21. G A Adegbola
22. J O Akinbo
23. S A Onoja
24. V I Nwalupue
25. C C Iweze
26. T A Abu
27. Charles K Amissah
28. F O Shusi
29. John
30. E Joseph
31. F A Onipede
32. R T Onyeje
33. E Okonkwo
34. J O O Osubu
35. A O Beckley
36. T Borha
37. G N Nwagwu
38. F A Harrison
39. F O Shoboyede
40. S Okandeji
41. J Babatunde
42. T Adisa
43. Q G Asouyah
44. B Atalaye
45. L E Odugo
46. I Nwaogu
47. A U Ikpe
48. D Openibo
49. F Oguegbunam
50. A Achilike
51. E Agbiboa
52. M Ozogolu

Obviously, I am missing some names in the above list because different accounts claim there were 68 students in the initial set of Finbarr's students. If Father Slattery was alive, he could have provided me an accurate list of the first set. Readers are encouraged to send me feedback on how to "correctize" the list in my future editions of my Finbarr's books. Yes, there will be future editions! At least, I am counting on it.

The first National President of SFCOBA, A. Madufor, came from FFS. The second National President was Tom Borha, an editor of Concord Group of Newspapers. The Third National President was M A C Odu, an Estate Surveyor and Valuer. SFCOBA accomplished a lot of things on behalf of Saint Finbarr's College. Land Surveying was conducted to establish the spatial limits of the school permanently. The order of Distinguished Conquerors (DC) was created to recognize distinguished alumni of the school. Tom Borha received the first one. I received the honor in 1998.

The Presidency of SFCOBA shifted from FFS in 1994 when Segun Ajanlekoko was elected. Segun quickly elevated SFCOBA and SFC into more national and international prominence through a variety of high-profile activities and projects. I met Segun around 1995 and we have both remained staunch advocates for SFC. The system of identifying students by their class years (sets) was established and advanced by SFCOBA. I belong to the 1972 Set.

When Mr. Yinka Bashorun became the national president, he instituted the process of unifying the various branches of SFCOBA domestically and abroad under one National and International SFCOBA. Everyone, to the last man, has been committed to the task of rekindling the glory days of Saint Finbarr's College.

The school made its first attempt at the West African School Certificate Examinations in 1961, having been approved in 1960. In that first attempt, the technical department had 100% passes, with 80% making 3 or 4 credits, while the Grammar, or basic as they were called, had 50% passes with two of them making distinctions. These boys were also at the top in sports and Vice-Admiral Patrick Koshoni (Retired) happens to be one of the two. From then on, the academic results kept improving year after year, with the technical department consistently recording 100% passes. In fact, in those days of Grade 1, Grade 2, and Grade 3 categorization of WAEC results, whenever the result was released, the understanding or common expectation was that all candidates would normally pass and what everybody was interested in was how many came out in Grade One or Grade Two: Grade Three was regarded as a consolation result. This trend remained true until the government takeover of schools in the mid 1970's.

Father Slattery placed a very high premium on discipline and could expel any student even if he was the best in academics or in football, once it was established that he had committed a serious offense. The gate used to be referred to as the gate of no return. There was no point in appealing a case of expulsion. Father Slattery never entertained such appeals – no pleading, no begging, and no beseeching. Saint Finbarr's College had four commandments, which constitute the Moral Pillars of the school.

(1) Any student caught stealing will be expelled.
(2) Any student caught copying during an examination time will be expelled.
(3) Any student caught leaving the school compound during school hours without the Principal's permission will be expelled.
(4) Any student caught smoking or with drugs will be expelled.

There was no in-between sanctions in the scale of punished. You are either retained or expelled. Period!

By the early 1970's Reverend Father Denis Joseph Slattery had a vision of making St. Finbarr's College all-encompassing in technical studies. He, therefore, decided to expand the technical workshops to cater both for the Senior and Junior Student. He introduced auto mechanics, electrical, and electronics departments. Two modern technical workshops were built from grants raised by his friends and overseas associates. The workshops were completed and fully equipped. They had hardly been used for two years when the government took over private schools in 1976. From 1976, the ideals for which Saint Finbarr's College was known, started to decline rapidly. Under government management, the school became over-populated and student indiscipline reigned. The decline reached a frightening level in the second half of the 1990's.

Fortunately, the government eventually deemed it wise to officially relinquish the takeover of private schools on the 2nd of October, 2001. Thus, Saint Finbarr's College started its second phase of academic advancement, alas without the all-encompassing presence of Father Slattery. By the time the school was returned to the Church, Father Slattery had diverted his attention to other pastoral pursuits. The return of the school took effect in 2003, after much educational damage has been done by the government. A furious academic cleansing ensued and many of the students who could not adjust were dismissed while those who could not stand the changes withdrew voluntarily. Consequently, by 2005, the enrolment at the school has gone down to a manageable level of 658 with the inherited "government students" constituting 413 students of the population. Below is a list of the noted principals of Saint Finbarr's College.

(1) Very Reverend Father Denis Joseph Slattery, Founding Principal, 1955-1975
(2) Late Anthony Omoera, 1975 to 1976
(3) Mr. A. A. Kpotie, 1977 to 1998
(4) Mr. Joseph Adusse, 1998 to 2001

The school has since been managed by a sequence of administrators from the Catholic Mission. Saint Finbarr's College has spread its tentacles around the world. Several "old boys" of the school are now in key productive and influential positions around the world. Like other notable high schools in Nigeria, Finbarr's has made significant contributions in human resource development in Nigeria. But one distinct and unmistakable fact about Finbarr's is that it has a unifying force – Reverend Father Denis Joseph Slattery (even after his death). The man and the name continue to strike a sense of refreshing chill in our hearts.

All graduates of Saint Finbarr's College remain very proud of the school's heritage. Father Slattery encouraged each person to embrace whatever his family religion dictated; but he demanded the study of the Bible as a source of well-rounded education. Thus, Bible Religious Studies was a core subject at the school. Father taught his students to enjoy the thrills and perils of playing sports as a preparation for the other challenges of life. The discipline received from the school has served us very well. It is probably the single most important factor in the professional and personal success of Saint Finbarr's

College "Old Boys." In the Yoruba language, Finbarrians are fondly referred to as "Omo Slattery," meaning Slattery's children. Yes, he was our father both in the figurative sense as well as in the spiritual sense.

Father Slattery trained us to be what we are and his lesson still lives on in every one of us. Although his service was primarily in Nigeria, his good example should be publicized to serve other parts of the world. To the last man, every Finbarrian (former and present) has the unity of purpose to disseminate the glory of Saint Finbarr's College, Akoka, Lagos, Nigeria.

St. Finbarr's College was named after Saint Finbarr of Cork City, Ireland. The narrative that follows is based partially on historical recollections of F. Ogundipe and supplemented by other student reports. The first stream of students in the college comprised 68 (sixty-eight) students in two classes of 34 students each. There were only four members of staff in the service of the school. Reverend Father Slattery, the principal, two teachers, and one office clerk, who was a seminarian. Two weeks after resumption from 21st January-10th February the school went on recess on account of the visit of Queen of England and Head of Commonwealth of Nations, who was visiting Nigeria at the time. The whole class of 1956 took part in the events culminating in Youth Day Parade at Race Course, Lagos in honor of the Queen. St. Finbarr's College bore the parade number 162. Classes resumed in the middle of February. Father Slattery himself taught English Language, Literature, Religious Knowledge and Latin. Mr. Bankole, now Chief Bankole taught General Science and Arithmetic, Algebra Geometry and Singing. Mr Ferdinand Ejike taught History and Geography. The first feast of Saint Finbarr, the patron saint of the school, was celebrated on 25th day of September, 1956 with Mass said by Father Slattery, with Openibo, Koshoni Jr and Ogundipe as mass servers.

Early accounts by FFS members indicate that the first interhouse sports festival of the school took place in 1956. That same founding year, SFC participated in Schools Table Tennis Championships with Jamogha, Ayeni and Wilson as Finbarr's stars. The first soccer match was played against host primary school, St. Paul's Primary School. Finbarr's lost 1-2 in an exciting game, which featured Paul Gborjoh alias P J Cobbler. Toward the end of 1956 another encounter was organized with Babies Team of St. Gregory's College, a sister school from where Father Slattery came to found Finbarr's.

In 1957, Finbarr's table tennis and soccer teams went over to Abeokuta to play Leonians. Messrs Henry Ekpeti and Ayo Adefolaju and G U M Nwagbara joined the teaching staff. Mr. Ekpeti taught Latin, Mr. Adefolaju taught Mathematics while Nwagbara taught History and Geography. Mr. Onabolu taught Fine Art. In 1958 Mr. Flyn came on staff from Ireland to teach Physics and Chemistry. Mr T C Nwosu, Mr Oweh and Mr. Oguike also joined the teaching staff. In January 1959, students moved to the permanent site at Akoka. The Bursar was Pa Adefuye, Head Laborer was Abu, Head of the new Department of Metalwork was Mr. Mooney. Mr. Flyn assumed Headship of Woodwork Department. Mr. Tommy joined during that year to take over teaching of English Language and Literature from Father Slattery. Mr. Omopariola joined to teach History. From 1960 the complement of staff was enlarged to include Mr. Drumm for Additional Mathematics, Elementary Mathematics and Physics; Mr. Mackenzie for Chemistry; Mr Omopariola for History; Mr. Oguike for Geography. Mr. Oguike left that year for further studies in USA; Mr. Nwagbara, who had left the previous year returned to teach History and Geogrpahy. Mr Nwosu left soon afterwards and Biology fell into the laps of Mr. Okpara before Mr. Nwajei arrived.

Finbarr's entered the Grier Cup competition in 1960. That year, the only qualifier, Eddy Akika, won the coveted Victor Ludorum Trophy winning Hurdles, Long Jump and coming second in High Jump event. Finbarr's entered the Zard Cup on June 2nd, 1960 and lost to St. Gregory's College 1-3. Mr. Drumm was Games Master, Alex Tolefe was Team Manager and Finbarr's Captain was Albert Alotey. On the 19th of June 1961 Finbarr's lost once more to St. Gregory's 0-1 in quarter final of the cup. The same day, Finbarr's was eliminated from the National Table Tennis Championship at Ibadan. Finbarr's lost at Semi Final Match 4-5 to Ansar U Deen College Isolo. Finbarr's stars were Heny Jamogha, Matin Adewusi, and Olusola John.

The first Zard Cup victory came in August 1962 when Finbarr's beat St. Gregorys's College 2-1 after an earlier 2-2 draw under the captainship of Jide Akinosoye (Akinzawelle). It is vital to recall the following : Patrick Koshoni who designed SFC badge unofficially in November 1956 on the blackboard. A proper school badge came in 1957. Jaamogha created the current shape of the badge in 1957 and Father Slattery approved it. Finbarr's lost a student, Pius Okifo, in 1957.

SFC van was purchased in 1959 and sprayed in school colors by Mr. Tommy. Ogundanna, a long-range runner was the first van conductor. Below is Ogundipe's own list of the foundation class of SFC.

1. F Ofili
2. B. Koshoni
3. P Koshoni
4. B Tevi
5. D Openibo
6. A Nwachukwu
7. D Johnson
8. F Ogundipe (the narrator)
9. S Assam
10. B Harrison
11. C Onyemenam
12. M Ozogolu
13. J Mathias
14. A Okpakpu
15. P Ezeah
16. P Gborjoh
17. A Oriakhi
18. F Adeniyi
19. G Bechi
20. P Adumekwe
21. E Uvwejomah
22. F Olafimihan,
23. Koffi
24. A Tolefe
25. E Okundayo
26. D Green
27. P Okonmah
28. S Ogundana
29. S Oguamana
30. A Mekwunye
31. A Beckley
32. S Salako
33. P Onipede,
34. G Uwagwu
35. L Rowland
36. M Okobi
37. T Borha
38. C Madufor
39. P Alade
40. F Wilson
41. J Awolowo
42. P Ojuriye
43. F Wilson
44. H Jamogha
45. A Jemade
46. G Ugba
47. A Coker
48. F Kotogbe
49. J Anighvo
50. J Egbuniwe
51. Sojinu
52. M Yaduat
53. C Igbonoba
54. A Bankole
55. C Omonikeji
56. F Adegburin
57. S Emeana
58. M Nwamara
59. A Nwago
60. F Rickets
61. A Adedipe
62. A Falola
63. A Ayeni
64. D Ojewande
65. G Adekoya
66. S Ibezim

Although not a perfect match, the above list compares well with the list presented earlier from another student source. As recollected by F. Ogundipe, tribes and tongues did not make any difference to anyone at Saint Finbarr's then, and they should not make any difference now. Other lists and accounts have been provided by several other Old Boys, including M. A. C. Odu. I did not make an attempt to reconcile the various lists of the First-Six students because, frankly, the lists are from different historical recollections and perspectives of the different early students and should be preserved as such. Even in the Bible, the Gospels by various Prophets are preserved as originally documented. In a non-computer era, all we can do is rely on the personal accounts and recollections of those offering testimonies. The government takeover of SFC probably led to the loss of crucial archival records of the early years of the college. Those records could have helped to authenticate each list.

Continuity of Excellence

After all these years, Saint Finbarr's College continues to excel in Academics, Sports, and Discipline. The school continues to receive accolades for its multi-dimensional accomplishments. In 2017, Business Day Research and Intelligence Unit (BRIU) published a guide to the best schools in Lagos, Nigeria. Saint Finbarr's College was listed among the topmost secondary schools in Lagos State. The school's performance in the West African Senior School Certificate Examinations since 2013 have been extraordinary. Based on the number of students who obtained five credits, including mathematics and English language, the pass rates have been 98.7 percent in 2013, 100 percent in 2014, 97.4 percent in 2015, 95 percent, in 2016, and 98.2 percent in 2017. Finbarr's students have been winning laurels at various academic competitions, including Helmbridge, Olympiad, Inter-collegiate Quiz and Debate, and so on. Academics has remained number one at Finbarr's!

In the same vein of superiority, Saint Finbarr's College won Soccer Guarantee Trust (GT) Bank Championship on June 29, 2017 at Onikan Stadium, Lagos, Nigeria. The school has expanded its sports excellence to include basketball, tennis, volleyball, and badminton. Sports excellence remains paramount at Finbarr's.

Of what use are academics and sports if there is no discipline? A high level of discipline is the avenue through which academic and sports potentials can be manifested. At Saint Finbarr's College, the virtues of discipline, self-control, respect, care for others, honesty, obedience, hard work, dedication, diligence, and resilience continue to be instilled in the students on a daily basis. In summary, Saint Finbarr's College provides a holistic education for its students. The biographical sketch of Father Slattery provided below is a fitting closure for this introduction chapter.

Biographical Summary of Reverend Father Denis Joseph Slattery

Father Slattery educated us in diverse ways so that we would be ready for the diverse challenges of the World. He, himself, engaged in diverse professional pursuits apart from being a priest. He was an educator, a lecturer, a teacher, an administrator, a newspaper editor, a columnist, a social activist, an orator, a soccer coach, a sports referee, and a boxer. He did it all with exceptional success and rave reviews.

Life's Timeline
Member of Society for Missions to Africa (SMA), effective June 29, 1936
Born February 29, 1916, Fermoy, in the diocese of Cloyne, Ireland
Entered priesthood on December 17, 1939
Died July 7, 2003 (Age 87), Saint Theresa Cork Hospital, Ireland
1941-1946, Vicariate of Benin, Nigeria
1947-1949 Catholic University, Washington, DC, USA
1949-1954 Vicariate of Lagos, Nigeria
1955-1999 Archdiocese of Lagos, Nigeria
1999-2003 Retirement, Blackrock Road Retirement Home, Cork, Ireland

Father Denis Joseph SLATTERY (1916 - 2003)
Denis Slattery was born in Fermoy, Co Cork, in the diocese of Cloyne, on 29th February 1916.

He died in St. Theresa's Unit, Blackrock Road, Cork, on 7th July 2003.

Denis was one of six boys and two girls born to Catherine (nee Curtin) and Timothy Francis Slattery. He was born the seventh child on the odd day of a leap year, that of 1916 – a momentous year for Ireland - both circumstances in which he took great relish. The family home was at 65 MacCurtain Street, Fermoy. Denis received his secondary education from the Christian Brothers in Fermoy (1928-1932) and at St Joseph's College, Wilton, matriculating in 1934. He was then promoted to the Society's Noviciate and house of philosophy at Kilcolgan, County Galway. Two years later he entered the Society's major seminary at Dromantine, Newry, County Down. Denis was received as a member of the Society on 29th June 1936. He was ordained to priesthood in St. Colman's Cathedral, Newry, by Bishop Edward Mulhern of Dromore diocese, on 17th December 1939. He was one of a group of seven ordained on that day.

After ordination Denis was appointed to the Vicariate of Bight of Benin, but because of the difficulties in obtaining a sea passage in wartime he did not reach Nigeria until May 1941. The convoy in which he travelled - the journey lasted thirty days - was bombed by German planes off L'Havre and a number of ships were sunk. On arrival Denis was assigned to Ilawe-Ekiti mission where he studied Yoruba. Six months later he was appointed to the staff of St. Gregory's College, Obalende, Lagos, Nigeria's first Catholic Secondary school, founded in 1928. On completion of two academic years – during which, in addition to his teaching work, he distinguished himself as Games Master – Denis was appointed Manager of St. Paul's Press and Bookshop at Ebute-Metta. He spent the last two years of his first missionary tour as Editor of the Nigerian Catholic Herald, based in Yaba. Denis' success in this latter capacity led his Superiors to send him to the Catholic University of America, Washington D.C. in January 1947. Taking Sociology, Journalism and Economics for his subjects he was awarded a Master of Arts degree by this institution in the summer of 1949. The title of his Masters thesis was 'The Transition from slavery to a free Labour Movement in Nigeria, 1850-1948'.

On his return to Nigeria in September 1949 Denis renewed his editorship of the Nigerian Catholic Herald. A monthly magazine when he first became editor, Denis turned the Herald into what he described as 'a militant anti-colonial religious and political weekly.' Indeed, this newspaper became important in molding public opinion in the lead up to Nigerian Independence bringing Denis into close and friendly contact with leading Nigerian Nationalists including Dr. Nnamdi Azikiwe. The Herald was particularly influential during the discussions on the Constitutional Conference. Denis also addressed social issues and his published extracts from his MA thesis relating to 'Nigerian Railways' Workers and the killing of the Coal Miners in Enugu', aroused considerable interest, while the fearlessness of his reports during the Nigerian Railways Strike of 1948-1949 earned him the plaudits of Nigerians and the hostility of the colonial government. In June 1954 Denis visited America on vacation and took time to raise funds for the Lagos jurisdiction. Six months later he returned to Nigeria. He was to remain in the Lagos jurisdiction until September 1999 when ill-health compelled him reluctantly to retire. In all he was to spend some fifty-five years in Nigeria, making him one of the longest-serving missionaries in the Society and one of two members of the Irish Province to give such service.

In 1955, Denis became founding principal of Saint Finbarr's College, which started as a two-classroom building on Apapa Road before moving to its present site at Akoka, Yaba. Denis was to guide this prestigious Grammar-cum-Technical school with a sure hand until 1976 when, with other Catholic schools, it was taken over by government. He devoted the remaining years of his missionary career to the pastoral ministry. He ministered in Saint Denis Catholic Church, Bariga-Akoka – near his beloved Saint Finbarr's, which he built and named. He also built and founded Saint Flavius Catholic Church, Oworonshoki, and Saint Gabriel's church, Somolu. In addition, he established Saint Joseph's Vocational School, and Our Lady of Fatima Nursery and Primary School, both in Akoka. In 1985, Denis was appointed Vicar General of Lagos Archdiocese, a post which required him to take charge of the jurisdiction during the Archbishop's absence.

Coming from a family keenly interested in sport, Denis' enthusiasm was given a very practical and important expression throughout his missionary career. In 1947, he became an accredited referee and a member of the Nigerian Association of Amateur Referees. He also pioneered the training of Nigeria's first indigenous referees. Despite his small stature, he radiated authority when in possession of the referee's whistle. As a FIFA-graded referee, he took charge of a number of international matches involving Nigeria and the Gold Coast (now Ghana) as well as many FA finals. He took a keen interest in schoolboy sport, helping to establish the popular school soccer competition, 'The Principal's Cup' (known popularly as the 'Zard Cup') in 1949. His own school, Saint Finbarr's, won this trophy in 1971, 1972 and 1973. Denis was also a member of the Nigerian Amateur Boxing Association. Moreover, putting his journalistic skills to good use, for many years he wrote a Sports Colum in the Lagos Weekend newspaper under the pen-name 'Green Flag'.

Denis received many honours during his life from the people he served so well. In 1989, he was conferred with chieftaincies by Imo State and Ile-Ife State. One of the chieftaincy titles fittingly hailed him as 'Enyi Oha 1 of Oru Ahiara Mbaise' ('Friend of the People'). The second title was that of 'Oosi Olokun-Ijio of Ife'. Denis's long and distinguished service was recognized by the Nigerian government in their National Honours Awards for 2001.

He received the Order of the Niger conferred on him during his retirement at Blackrock Road. A year later he was also to be honoured by the Fermoy Urban Council.

In 1996, to commemorate his 80th birthday, Denis published his memoirs under the title "My Life Story," at the urge of a group of his former students from Saint Finbarr's College. This was launched at the Institute of International Affairs, Kofo Abayomi, Victoria Island, Lagos. His age and status allowed him to speak openly on social, religious, and political issues and he was widely reported. From the 1960's he was known as a staunch advocate and encouraging critic of the people of Nigeria in their search for self-expression and self-reliance as a nation.

Denis celebrated the Golden Jubilee of his priesthood in 1989 and his Diamond Jubilee in 1999. The homilist at his funeral Mass said: 'There is no doubt that Denis took great pride in all his achievements. But his life was ultimately lived not to bring honour to himself but to give honour and glory to God.'

Thus, closed the chapter of the life of a magnificent man, a lover of humanity, and a servant of the society.

Biographical Sketch of the Author

Professor Adedeji Bodunde Badiru (1952 -) is an ex-Finbarrian, having attended Saint Finbarr's College from 1968 to 1972, of which he remains everlastingly proud. Professor Badiru is presently a Professor of Systems Engineering and also SES-level Dean of the Graduate School of Engineering and Management at the Air Force Institute of Technology (AFIT). He has oversight for planning, directing, and controlling operations related to granting doctoral and master's degrees, professional continuing cyber education, and research and development programs for the US Air Force. He was previously Professor and Head of Systems Engineering and Management at AFIT, Professor and Department Head of Industrial Engineering at the University of Tennessee - Knoxville, and Professor of Industrial Engineering and Dean of University College at the University of Oklahoma, Norman. He is a registered professional engineer (PE), a certified Project Management

Professional (PMP), a Fellow of the Institute of Industrial & Systems Engineers, and inducted as a Fellow of the Nigerian Academy of Engineering in 2006. Professor Badiru is also an ABET Program Evaluator (PEV), for worldwide accreditation evaluations of engineering and technology academic programs. He holds a leadership certificate from the University Tennessee Leadership Institute. He has BS in Industrial Engineering, MS in Mathematics, and MS in Industrial Engineering from Tennessee Technological University, and Ph.D. in Industrial Engineering from the University of Central Florida. His areas of interest include mathematical modeling, project modeling and analysis, economic analysis, systems engineering modeling, computer simulation, and productivity analysis. He is a prolific author, with over 35 books, over 35 book chapters, over 135 Journal and magazine articles, and over 200 conference presentations. He is a member of several professional associations and scholastic honor societies.

Professor Badiru, a world-renowned innovative educator, has won several awards for his teaching, research, administrative, and professional accomplishments. Some of his selected awards include the 2009 Dayton Affiliate Society Council Award for Outstanding Scientists and Engineers in the Education category with a commendation from the 128th Senate of Ohio, 2010 ASEE John Imhoff Award for his global contributions to Industrial Engineering Education, the 2011 Federal Employee of the Year Award in the Managerial Category from the International Public Management Association, Wright Patterson Air Force Base, the 2012 Distinguished Engineering Alum Award from the University of Central Florida, the 2012 Medallion Award from the Institute of Industrial Engineers for his global contributions in the advancement of the profession, 2016 Outstanding Global Engineering Education Award from the Industrial Engineering and Operations Management (IEOM), 2015 Air Force-level Winner of the National Public Service Award from The American Society for Public Administration and the National Academy of Public Administration, 2013 Father D. J. Slattery Excellence Award, Saint Finbarr's College Alumni Association, North America Chapter, 2013 Award Team Leader, Air Force Organizational Excellence Award for Air University C3 (Cost Conscious Culture), 2013 Finalist for Jefferson Science Fellows Program, National Academy of Sciences, 2012 Book-of-the-Month Recognition for Statistical Techniques for Project Control from the Industrial Engineering Magazine, and the 2010 and 2020 Industrial Engineering Joint

Publishers Book-of-the-Year Awards for The Handbook of Military Industrial Engineering and The Story of Industrial Engineering.

Professor Badiru is also the book series editor for CRC Press/Taylor & Francis book series on Systems Innovation. He has served as a consultant to several organizations around the world including Russia, Mexico, Taiwan, Nigeria, and Ghana. He has conducted customized training workshops for numerous organizations including Sony, AT&T, Seagate Technology, U.S. Air Force, Oklahoma Gas & Electric, Oklahoma Asphalt Pavement Association, Hitachi, Nigeria National Petroleum Corporation, and ExxonMobil. He has served as a Technical Project Reviewer, curriculum reviewer, and proposal reviewer for several organizations including The Third-World Network of Scientific Organizations, Italy, Social Sciences and Humanities Research Council of Canada, National Science Foundation, National Research Council, and the American Council on Education. He is on the editorial and review boards of several technical journals and book publishers. Prof. Badiru has also served as an Industrial Development Consultant to the United Nations Development Program. In 2011, Prof. Badiru led a research team to develop analytical models for Systems Engineering Research Efficiency (SEER) for the Air Force acquisitions integration office at the Pentagon. He has led a multi-year composite manufacturing collaborative research between the Air Force Institute of Technology and KBRWyle Aerospace Group. Prof. Badiru has diverse areas of avocation. His professional accomplishments are coupled with his passion for writing about everyday events and interpersonal issues, especially those dealing with social responsibility. Outside of the academic realm, he writes motivational poems, editorials, and newspaper commentaries; as well as engaging in paintings and crafts.

On the basis of his global and wide span of personal and professional accomplishments, Professor Badiru was inducted into the prestigious rank of Distinguished Conqueror (DC) of Saint Finbarr's College Alumni in October 1998.

Chapter One References

1. Badiru, Adedeji, *The Story of Saint Finbarr's College: Father Slattery's Contributions to Education and Sports in Nigeria,* iUniverse, Bloomington, Indiana, USA, 2018

2. Badiru, Adedeji, *Blessings of a Father: Education contributions of Father Slattery at Saint Finbarr's College,* iUniverse, Bloomington, Indiana, USA, 2013.

3. Badiru, Adedeji., *Blessings of a Father: A Tribute to the Life and Work of Reverend Father Denis Joseph Slattery,* Heriz Designs and Prints, Lagos, Nigeria, 2005.

4. Slattery, Denis J (1996), *My Life Story,* West African Book Publishers, Limited, Ilupeju, Lagos, Nigeria, 1996.

Chapter Two

Academics at Saint Finbarr's College

As a personal testimonial, the high school academics at Saint Finbarr's College prepared me very well for the challenges of university studies in the USA. Even today, I can still look back and admire the soundness of Finbarr's academic preparation. When I travelled overseas to the USA in 1975, I brought my Finbarr's class notebooks in Physics, Chemistry, Biology, Mathematics, and French with me. I still occasionally flip through the pages of the notes to marvel at the depth of learning that we, the students, accomplished as Saint Finbarr's College. What makes it even more astonishing is the fact that we did what we did with meager academic resources, compared with what High School kids of today enjoy. As an example, to the delight and wonderment of my university instructors, I excelled in my undergraduate Chemistry classes at Tennessee Technological University in 1976, directly on the basis of the incoming knowledge that I already had from Finbarr's. One of the Chemistry graduate students was a Nigerian named Victor Folarin, who later became a medical doctor and served in the USA Air Force medical service. He rose to the rank of Colonel in the Air Force. As a Chemistry graduate teaching assistant, he oversaw our Chemistry lab experiments. He was amazed how a new foreign student from Nigeria could readily outshine even the American students in the classes. He was proud to tell everyone that he and I were from the same country. This is all because of the academic preparation from Saint Finbarr's College. In fact, I used my Finbarr's notebooks to supplement the university lectures. Many of the topics covered in Physics and Chemistry at the university level were the same topics that we already covered at the high school level at Saint Finbarr's College. Finbarr's academics gave me an academic edge at the university level. The front covers of my Finbarr's notebooks, which I manually and artistically designed, continue to be a product of pride for me. Figures 4 through 6 show the notebook covers. The notebooks have been elevated to the level of being classics and worthy of being a collector's items.

Figure 4. Cover Image of Physics Notebook

Figure 5. Cover Image of Chemistry Notebook

Figure 6. Cover Image of Biology Notebook

In the pages of these notebooks reside tremendous academic treasures that I still cherish very much today. Because of my artistic stills and interest, I was the classroom illustrator in my Finbarr's Biology class. I drew illustrations on the blackboard for other students to copy onto their own notebooks. Many times, my classmates borrowed my notebooks to take home for the copying chore, if they could not finish their drawing during the classroom session. The graphics-drawing skills that I developed at Saint Finbarr's College continue to serve me well even in today's digital age. Samples of my biology illustrations are shown in the Figures 7 through 14.

Figure 7. Biology Illustration 1

Figure 8. Biology Illustration 2

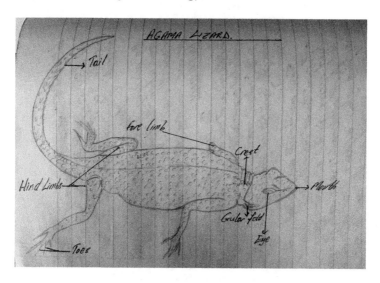

Figure 9. Biology Illustration 3

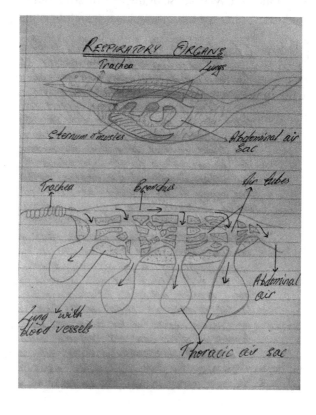

Figure 10. Biology Illustration 4

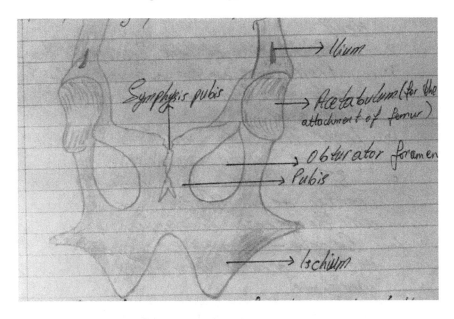

Figure 11. Biology Illustration 11

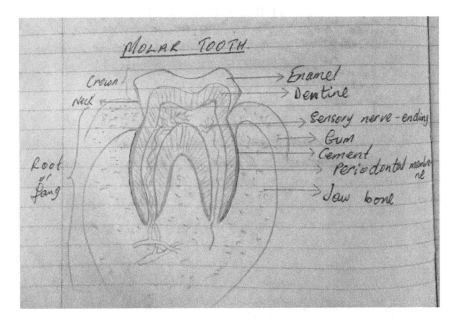

Figure 12. Biology Illustration 12

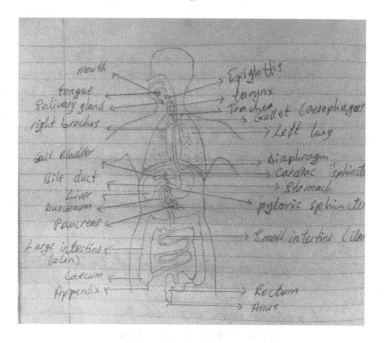

Figure 13. Biology Illustration 13

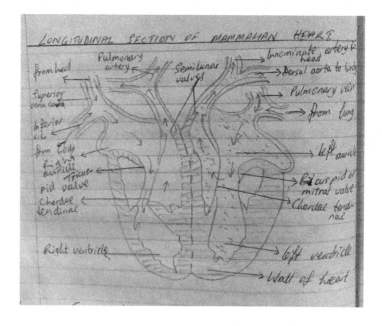

Figure 14. Biology Illustration 14

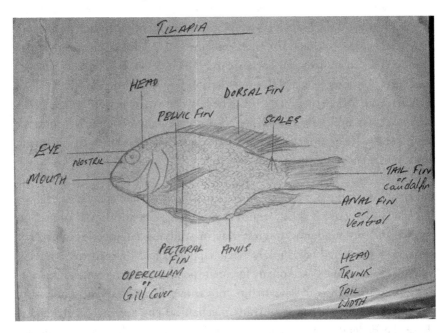

My proficiency in doing classroom biology illustrations was the reason many of my classmates, teachers, Father Slattery, friends, neighbors, and family expected me to go on to study medicine. I, indeed, secured a government scholarly later on to study medicine, but engineering was my dream profession. I did the biology illustrations because of my personal passion for drawing, graphic designs, and artistic pursuits, for which our art teacher, in his own view, thought I should go on to study Fine Arts. At the same time, the English language teacher opined that I should become a writer. This has been manifested, as documented by my many recreational publications, but not as a professional writer in the context that he envisioned.

Based on my Finbarr's lecture notes illustration experience, my artistic skills were also called upon while I was working as a Graphic Artist at the Audio-Visual Aids Section of the Lagos State Ministry of Education, where I did hand-drawn illustrations for educational television programs for elementary schools in 1973. So, I can claim that I was involved in on-air, online, or distance learning education programs well before they became popular nowadays with modern technology.

I also did well in French language, which led to the reason that my French teacher, Mr. Akinrimade, insisted that I should go into foreign service because of my aptitude for the French language. He later joined the military and went on to teach at the National Defense Academy (NDA) in Kaduna, from where he invited me to compete for entrance to NDA in 1973. I did attend the one-week selection interview at NDA for the 15th Regular Admission Exercise in Kaduna from 24th September 1973. The basis of my invitation for the NDA interview was my performance in NDA's nationally-competitive entrance examination. I was reported as having the best NDA Entrance Examination result in the entire Lagos State at that time.

By chance during the interview week, I ran into a former elementary school classmate, Dankaiye Kabiru, who was already a cadet at NDA at time. But, once again, my academic interest was in studying engineering abroad. I sometimes wondered what might have happened had I joined the Nigerian military at that time. Based on my fortunate good academic records, I was able to secure admissions and scholarships for various disciplines. One scholarship was to go to East Germany to study mechanical engineering. In the end, I chose the Federal Government scholarship to study industrial engineering at Tennessee Technological University in Cookeville, Tennessee, USA. The Figures 15 through 17 illustrate my academic performance and records from Saint Finbarr's College. My West African Examination Council (WAEC) result was in Grade I Distinction, which attracted a lot of attention for employment and academic progression. When the WAEC result came out, Father Slattery, being ever the braggart of academics that he was, sent a junior student, Joe Ugbegua, to deliver the good news from the school to my neighborhood at Apapa Road, Ebute Metta. Being a close-knit community, the whole neighborhood was in a fever pitch with the excitement of the good news. Joe Ugbegua later became an Engineering Manager at Total Nigeria, Plc. This is another demonstration of the technical reaches of Finbarr's. My love of reading and writing, honed at Saint Finbarr's College, still continues today. I maintained my Yaba-Lagos public library card (Figure 18) for many years, even after departing to the USA for further studies. My student ID card from Saint Finbarr's College is shown in Figure 19.

Figure 15. WAEC Examination Result

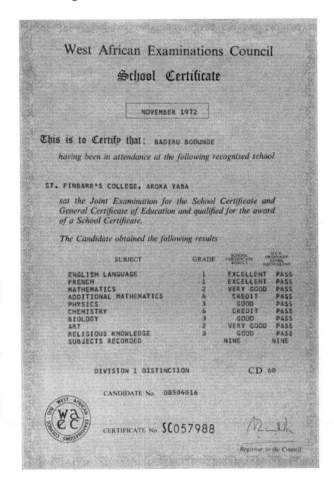

Figure 16. Finbarr's Recommendation

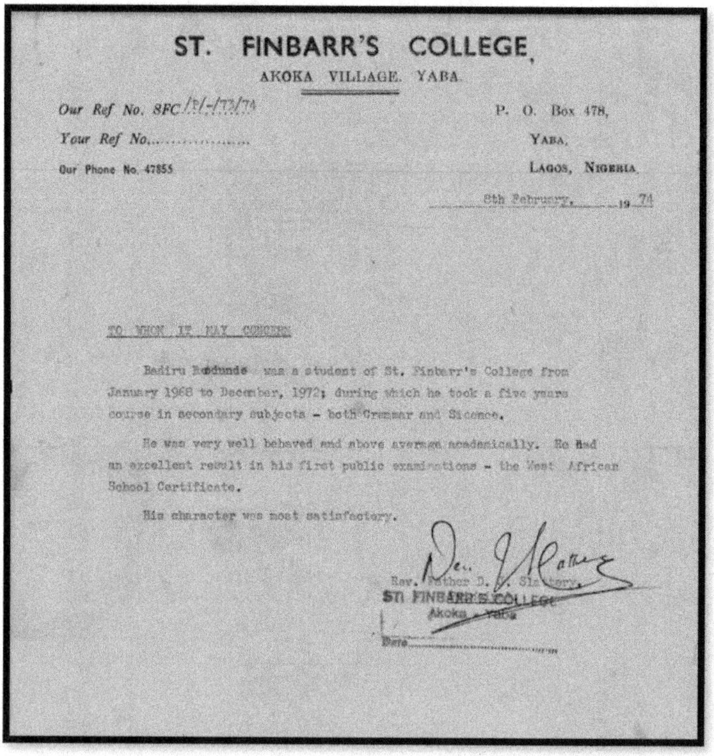

ST. FINBARR'S COLLEGE,
AKOKA VILLAGE, YABA.

Our Ref No. SFC/B/-/73/74
Your Ref No.................
Our Phone No. 47855

P. O. Box 478,
YABA,
LAGOS, NIGERIA.

8th February, 19 74

TO WHOM IT MAY CONCERN:

Badiru Badunde was a student of St. Finbarr's College from January 1968 to December, 1972; during which he took a five years course in secondary subjects - both Grammar and Science.

He was very well behaved and above average academically. He had an excellent result in his first public examinations - the West African School Certificate.

His character was most satisfactory.

Rev. Father D. [illegible] Slattery.
ST. FINBARR'S COLLEGE
Akoka - Yaba
Date.................

Figure 17. Finbarr's Testimonial

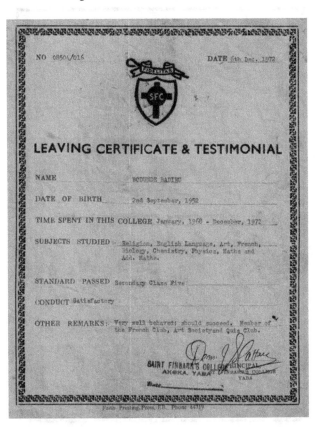

Figure 18. Library Card

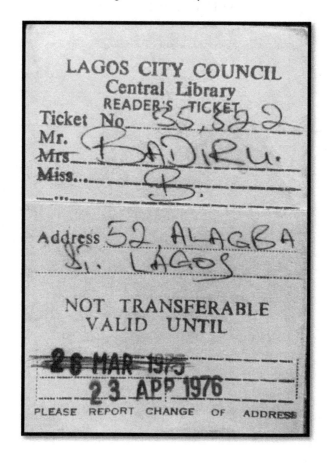

Figure 19. Finbarr's Student ID Card

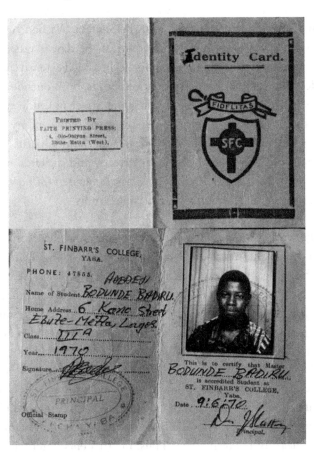

My Fortuitous Journey to Saint Finbarr's College

My admission to Finbarr's was a textbook case example of the ideals of academics at Saint Finbarr's College. It was serendipity at its best. In order to understand how Saint Finbarr's College transformed my life, one needs to know my own beginning and early years and how I came to cross paths with Reverend Father Slattery. I overcame several adversities before reaching my present educational attainment and professional accomplishments.

I was born on September 2nd, 1952, into the Sharafa Ola Badiru Onisarotu family of Epe, Lagos State. By the standard of the day, it was an affluent family. My father was a building contractor and traveled extensively in pursuit of his profession. Several of his children were, thus, born outside of Epe. He was a particularly popular person at Okegbogi Street in Ondo township in the late 1940s and early 1950s. I was only five years old when my father died prematurely on April 12, 1958. Thus, began the family hiatus that would disrupt what would have otherwise been a steady and sheltered upbringing. Because of his sudden death, his family was not prepared for how to manage and care for the younger children in the large family.

Fortunately, we had some grown children among us at that time. The adult children in the family "distributed" the younger ones among themselves to see to their upbringing. In the process, I was shuttled from one place to another, from one sibling to another, and from one extended relative to another. Over a period of a few years, I stayed with brothers, sisters, uncles, and some distant relatives. I had the good fortune of having a large and extended family with no shortage of good Samaritans willing to take me on as a ward.

The result of being a migrant ward was that I could not start school until 1961 — at the late age of nine! I started elementary school as Zumratul Islamiyyah Elementary school at No. 2, Tawaliu Bello Street, adjacent to Nnamdi Azikwe Road in the heart of Lagos in 1961. Thus, my first encounter with counting 1, 2, 3 and reciting A, B, C was not until I was nine years old. This late start, coupled with the fact that I started school in Lagos, where primary education was for eight years (in those days) compared to six years in the Western region, meant that I was five years behind my educational cohorts. But one thing that was in my favor at that time was my maturity level. At that age, I already understood the importance of education. I did not need any prodding or forcing to go to school. My level of maturity made me more attentive and appreciative of the teachers in the classroom, so; I was able to take in all lessons presented by the teachers. I did not need any supplementary lessons outside of school. In those days, teachers and observers erroneously attributed my better school performance (compared to my classmates) to my higher level of intelligence. For a long time, I mistakenly believed it too. But what was actually fueling the better academic performance was my higher maturity level. I enjoyed excellent rapport with my classmates and teachers. I could tell that the teachers not only liked me, but also respected me. For this reason, I never got into any punishment episode at school. I went through the entire elementary school without ever being flogged at school, in an age when school flogging was very rampant. The same record was later repeated throughout my secondary school years.

I suffered enough flogging at the homes of my guardians (for being rascally) to make up for the grace that I enjoyed at school. Contrary to the typical situation in those days, the school was my refuge. I enjoyed going to school in order to escape what I considered to be very oppressive disciplinary home environment. It happened that what, as a child, I considered to be oppressive chores at home turned out to be valuable lessons that still continue to serve me well at home until today. I still remain very handy at home, particularly in the kitchen and general household chores. My adoption of school as a refuge was fortuitous because it paved the way for my sound academic foundation. I knew I would not be able to study at home so I paid every bit of attention to the lectures at school. That way, I imbibed everything the teacher had to say. I never had an opportunity for supplementary lessons or studying at home. I relied entirely on school lectures. I could not afford not to pay attention at school. Children nowadays have the luxury of private lessons. Sometimes they get too lackadaisical about the opportunities.

In those days, I tended to have a free-wheeling lifestyle of freedom to roam the neighborhood streets in search of play and fun. This did not sit well with my guardians, who preferred for me to be indoors to attend to household chores. So, I was frequently on a collision course with my guardians about my over-commitment to playing around the neighborhood. In spite of this rascally disposition, I still enjoyed good relationships with my guardians primarily because I still performed well in school. I recall an elderly neighbor intervening and pleading with one of my guardians to spare me a flogging on account of my school performance. He opined that, in spite of my playing too much, I was still doing very well at school compared to my playmates, who were playing and not doing well at school.

One of my favorite guardians was my uncle, the late Chief Alao Shabi. I learnt a lot of calm demeanor and rational mode of speaking from him. Although he flogged me a few times also, it was always at the instigation of unfair reports getting to him about what and what offense I had committed. Typical reports were about my being seen riding a bicycle around the neighborhood, swimming in a local public pool, or playing football on the playground. These were all considered dangerous and unauthorized acts in those days. That some of us learnt to ride bicycles, swim, and play football was a credit to our mischievous acts of running away from home for a few hours to engage in these fun but "dangerous" acts. My uncle was a scrap-metal dealer. He had a scrap-metal shop at Idumagbo in the heart of Lagos in the 1960s. His shop was later moved to Owode Onirin in the outskirts of Lagos. From 1965 through 1967, I helped him to tend the scrap metal shop along with his Hausa assistant, named Gaji. The general expectation was that after elementary school, I would become a full-time apprentice to my uncle and eventually go into the scrap metal business, which was a lucrative business in those days. My uncle engaged in exporting scrap metals overseas. So, he interacted with white expatriates through the ports at Apapa. The decades following Nigeria's independence saw a decline in the lucrative level of scrap metals. If I had gone into that business, I would probably be mired in the economic depression associated with it now.

I learnt a lot of hands-on activities from Gaji. He was the one who first introduced me to the properties of various metals and how to handle them. He gave me an early (albeit unscientific) appreciation for various metals. We sorted scrap metals into their respective categories. We dealt with mercury, silver, iron, steel, copper, brass, platinum, and other metals. I don't recall handling gold in those days. The hands-on skills still serve me well today in handling household tools. Even now, my most cherished possessions are the implements of household work such as hammers, pliers, screw drivers, drills, and so on. Anyone visiting my home now can hardly miss my intimate relationships with these implements.

I graduated from elementary school in 1967 and was to enter secondary school in January 1968. Because of my good academic performance and excellent result in the common entrance examination, it was generally believed that I would not encounter any difficulty in gaining admission into a secondary school. But there were other obstacles lurking beneath the raw academic record. What I thought should not matter in gaining admission into a reputable school (befitting of my common entrance results) were actually major obstacles in the eyes of the secondary school officials.

The prospects of not being able to pay school fees preempted my being admitted to the most reputable secondary schools. My sister, the late Mrs. Omowunmi Ayodele Durosimi (previously Mrs. Shojobi), insisted that I must go to a reputable high school because of her belief and confidence in my academic promise. She had monitored my performance throughout my elementary school and concluded that nothing but the best schools were appropriate for me. She, herself, had attended Queens School, Ede, in the Western Region. She had the vision of my attending such schools such as Kings College, Government College, and other well-known schools. Well, I applied to all those schools. Based on my common entrance examination results, I was invited for interview at all the schools. I was self-assured and confident about my academic-related performance at the interviews. But I was naïve about the other factors that were considered in admitting children to those schools. Frequently, at those interviews, I had no shoes on and wore the simplest of clothes. Being more mature than the other kids seeking admission, I always attended the interviews by myself. No accompanying parents, siblings, or relatives. If I had asked my family members, I could have received appropriate support to put on an "air" of being well-off enough to attend the schools. But I made a deliberate and conscious decision to attend the interview just as I was – without any pretensions. I was somehow arrogant about my academic capabilities, and I believed the school authorities would be impressed. But I was very wrong. My attitude going into the interviews was that I wanted to challenge the interviewers to ask me any question about school subjects so that I could impress them with my knowledge. But very often, questions were raised only about tangential elements that had nothing to do with school subjects. Some typical questions that I faced (and failed) were:

Who will pay your school fees?
Where is your father's house?

Did your mother attend a secondary school?

Has anybody in your family attended this school before?

Is your mother a trader or a government worker?

What is your professional goal?

Which elementary school did you attend?

Have you ever attended a nursery school?

The interviewers thought I would be a misfit at an Ivy-League type of secondary school. Although Zumratul Islamiyyah Elementary School was a good school on the inside, it was not highly regarded externally. This could be because it was located in the rough and tough inner-city part of Lagos Island. The street address of No. 2 Tawaliu Bello Street, adjacent to Nnamidi Azikwe Road, was noted more for commercial activities rather than as an academic base for a well-regarded school. The school had since been demolished and the site had been designated for other commercial purposes.

I had no doubt the other kids had been well-coached about the interview questions and had well-honed answers for all such silly questions. But I was brash and determined not to stoop too low as to give answers that would amount to pretensions. My sister had expected that many schools would be so impressed with my academic performance that they would admit me with scholarship offers. So, there was no prior arrangement or preparation by my family regarding how to pay my school fees. Frankly, my sister was caught off guard by the disappointing admission outcomes.

To be somewhat fair to the interviewers, my older age probably played against me. There I was trying to enter a secondary school at the ripe age of 16. I was five years older than my contemporaries seeking admission at the same time. Not knowing my history of starting school very late (at the age of 9), the interviewers very likely equated my advanced age to being slow in the elementary school. Their natural suspicion of my being academically dim did not match the documented performance on paper. So, they probably decided to err on the side of caution.

Zumratul did not have a secondary school at that time. Otherwise, I would have been a shoo-in to progress from Zumratul Elementary School to Zumratul Secondary School. So, I was like a goldfish out of a backyard pond looking to be placed in an ivy-league aquarium.

That I even attended Zumratul Elementary School had been by accident rather than by design. At my age of nine years in 1961, elementary schools were reluctant to enroll me. I was a raw and untested pupil with no prior preparation to enter school. The "raw" part of me at that time was what led to my moniker of "BB Raw-Raw" later on. BB stands for my middle and last names – Bodunde Badiru. I proudly autographed that insignia on my early drawings and paintings. The full salutation was "BB Raw-Raw, Broken Bottle Never Tires," whatever that was supposed to mean, I never knew. Many of my early friends still call me BB; but most people have forgotten or never knew of the Raw-Raw part of the motto.

In the search for my first elementary school, it happened that a sister-in-law, the late Mrs. Shadiyat Badiru, wife of my late brother, Mr. Atanda Badiru, was a book seller at the school at the time that an elementary school was being sought for me. She took me to the principal, who queried me about why I was just entering school for the first time. I was able to give him satisfactory answers because I was old enough to be cognizant of my situation and the consequences of my predicament. The principal was very impressed with my mature communication abilities. He decided to enroll me, jokingly making a comment that "Enu e dun," which satirically meant that my stories were tantalizing.

In 1967, I was invited to several Secondary School admission interviews. Notable among these were King's College, Lagos and Government College, Ibadan. None of these were successful. Even though the interview experiences were not successful, they were, nonetheless, very gratifying. The honor of being invited to interview at those schools brought much pride and joy to the officials of my elementary school. The interview at Government College, Ibadan, was a protracted one-week affair that culminated in written and oral tests on various subjects. I was informed that I did very well on the tests but did not meet the cut-off requirements in the overall interview. I returned to Lagos empty-handed.

One theme that because obvious in many of the interview at these highly-coveted schools were social-elitist questions similar to the sample below:

"Who are you?"
"Who is your father?"

"Where does your father work?"

"Whom do you know in government?"

"What are your family assets?"

"Who in your family has attended this school before?"

"What social affiliations does your family have?"

"What is your neighborhood like?"

"Do you know any high-ranking civil servant?"

"Who will pay your school fees?"

"Where do you normally spend your holidays?"

Of course, I didn't have the right answer for any of such questions. So, it was obvious that I did not belong, in spite of my superior academic performance. I answered such questions truthfully, thinking that the answer did not matter. What should matter was my academic records. I was naively wrong!

I was intent on not allowing my academic potential to go to waste, even though I was convinced that I would do well in any non-education-based career that I might end up with. After attending several high-school admission interviews and not being successful, I concluded that I needed a better answer to the question of "Who will pay your school fees?" So, I embarked on an effort of seeking financial support from local philanthropists. One noted person that I appealed to was the late Chief S. B. Bakare. I had heard of several philanthropic projects that he had undertaken. I was hopeful that he would be so impressed by my academic potential that he might want to invest in my education. So, I crafted a well-written letter to him explaining my plight. The letter included carefully composed paragraphs that would indicate to him my knowledge and command of the English language, even at that age. I included statements about my common entrance exam results. I never received a response.

My disappointment was contained only by the prospects of contacting other philanthropists in Lagos. There was no shortage of such benefactors in Lagos in those days. Unfortunately, none of them came my way. All my attempts at pursuing philanthropic grace were futile. Years later, I began to understand why I might not have heard from those that I contacted. It could have been that they never received my letters at all because I did not have the correct addresses. It could also have been that their administrative assistants obstructed the delivery of the letters. Perhaps, they received thousands of requests, beyond what they could comfortably respond to or provide financial assistance for.

My admission to Saint Finbarr's College was nothing short of a miracle that manifested itself through the hands of Father Slattery. After several months on searching for a secondary school without success, the family's attention turned to exploring other options for my future. There were discussions of my going into some trade apprenticeship. A popular option was for me to capitalize on my drawing skills by going into a sign-writing business. Imagine the caption, "BB Raw-Raw Signs" or "BB, the Sign Writer" on a roadside kiosk.

That Saint Finbarr's College was considered as an option was due to a fortunate act of geographical proximity. I was living with my sister at the University of Lagos Staff Quarters at that time. She was then married to Dr. Wole Shojobi, who was then a Civil Engineering lecturer at the University. Having found no school yet, my sister decided that we should consider one of the local schools on the mainland of Lagos. Thus, Saint Finbarr's College came into the picture. Being in the immediate vicinity of Unilag, Finbarr's was a convenient choice.

The school was appealing because it was nearby and did not have a boarding school. Attending a boarding school far away would have compounded my financial inability to pay the school fees. My sister contacted Saint Finbarr's College and found out that there might be some openings in the school. It was already two weeks after school session started in January 1968. The fact that any openings existed at that time was a fortuitous coincidence. The school was looking for a few additional good students and I was looking for one good school. My sister sent me to the school to inquire. As usual, I went to the school all by myself.

It was a good thing that Reverend Father Slattery did not care what a prospective student looked like. I went to the school without shoes and no impressive "garmentry." Unlike my previous secondary school interview experiences, Father Slattery attended to me the same way he attended to all the parents who had come to the school with their kids to inquire about the "rumoured" openings. The Father was quite an impressive and blessed being. Although it was the first time that I would speak directly to a white man, I completely understood him and he understood me perfectly. I believe this

51

is a credit to his years of living in Nigeria and communicating with various categories of Nigerians in local communities. He announced to everyone that there were **only three** vacancies. He cautioned that no parent should approach him to lobby for the open positions. He was going to fill the three vacancies purely on the basis of merit. There were several parents and kids in the audience when the announcement was made. I was the only unaccompanied boy in the group. By my own estimate, there must have been at least two hundred boys. I concluded that I had no chance, and presumed this to be another disappointing outcome in my lengthy and lonely search for a secondary school.

How was Father Slattery going to ensure a fair process of selecting only three kids from the hundreds that were interested in being admitted? He laughed at the parents' inquiry. He responded that he had an ingenious plan. He told everyone to come back on some specified date. He did not say what the selection plan was. I believe he kept the plan secret to preempt any attempt by any parent to usurp the process. Without knowing the selection process, no one knew how to prepare or scheme for success. He told everyone there was no need for the kids to prepare anything for the appointed date. Just show up on time. Disappointed, everyone left for that day. I was filled with misgivings about the whole thing. But I was heartened by the fact that I was still in the running.

On the appointed day, I showed up at the school, unaccompanied, as usual. Father Slattery told everyone to assemble in the open field across from the Assembly Hall. There were hundreds of anxious eyes. There were murmurings among the parents regarding what was going on; and what was going to happen. Father Slattery stepped onto the high concrete pavement bordering the Assembly Hall. This position gave him an elevated view of the audience. It was like being on a high-rise podium. After positioning himself majestically in front of and above the audience, he announced that he was going to select three kids from the audience to fill the open vacancies on the basis of the common entrance exam results. Everyone was baffled. How was he going to do that? Father asked two clerks from the school office to come onto the pavement. A table and a chair were hurriedly positioned on the pavement. The clerks had been inside the Assembly Hall (as if on a secret mission), waiting for Father's instruction to emerge. After the clerks were appropriately settled, with one sitting on the chair and the other standing beside the table with papers and pencils in hand, Father Slattery beckoned to the school secretary, I believe her name was Monica, to bring out a big pile of typed sheets, the like of which I had never seen until then. The pile must have measured almost one foot above the table. People in the audience looked at one another anxiously. No one knew what was about to unfold.

As I would become aware later on during my days at Saint Finbarr's, Father Slattery's antics at getting things done often bordered on craziness. He was a renegade of a person. He had a penchant for the unexpected. His ways of doing things were replete with surprises, wonderment, curiosity, and suspense. He could have been a successful movie star.

He would always find unusual and amusing ways to get things done. I think that was by a deliberate design by him. Through his unconventional approach, he got a lot of attention. Once he got your attention, he could then impose his will on you. People were often amused, rather than being offended, by his unusual and eccentric ways. He had a volatile temperament to match his odd ways. But no one dared challenge him. So, everyone waited patiently for him to announce his grand plan. He hesitated in announcing his plan deliberately to keep the audience in suspense and partly to disarm any rancor from the audience. Father Slattery often operated like a shrewd psychologist. He had all kinds of ingenious means of dealing with people. That was why he was so beloved throughout Nigeria. I don't think he ever lost an argument in his heydays. When discussions didn't go his way, he would put on a fake tantrum in order to still get his way. People usually succumbed to him by simply laughing in amazement of his antics. He was an all-encompassing person: a Revered Clergyman, a comic (if need be), a humorist (if necessary to lighten the moment), a runner (chasing after mischievous kids), a boxer (if needed to mete out a punishment), and a sportsman to the core. Except for his clergy robes, his restless ways revealed no sign that he was a Catholic priest. It was not until his later years, in a slowed state of physical being, that anyone could rein him in.

Well, with all the suspense over, Father Slattery announced that the clerks would start reading names off the pile of common entrance examination results. The pile of computer paper contained the list of common entrance results in merit order. Names would be read from the list until the three highest scoring boys in the audience were identified. This process was baffling because there was no way to ensure when the three names would be found among those kids in the audience. Father maintained that if all the kids in the audience had taken the common entrance examination in Lagos State, then their names would appear somewhere in the list of results, even if they were at the far end of the list. Father Slattery said he was prepared to continue this exercise until the highest three had been identified, even if it took days. Being enmeshed in the crowd, I could hear hisses from some parents. Were they prepared to commit that kind of indefinite time, with no assurance of success in the end? Some parents tried to get Father's attention for private discussions. But he refused. Even the highly-placed, obviously rich, and well-connected parents in the audience could not sway Father Slattery from his determined approach. Many parents tensely tried to explain the process to their kids. Being alone, I had no one to explain anything to me. Instead, I eavesdropped on the covert mumblings deep within the recesses of the crowd.

Unconcerned, Father Slattery motioned to the clerks to start reading out the names. So it was that we embarked on this journey of the seemingly endless reading of names. I started praying fervently inwardly to be one of the three selected. Being of small stature, and having only myself to account for, I gradually pushed my way to the front of the crowd. I positioned myself right in front of the clerks' table. I was occasionally pushed back by one of the clerks, wanting to create sufficient elbow room for the prevailing task. At one time, Father Slattery threatened to end the process if the audience crowded the clerks too closely. But realizing the anxiety among the audience, he relented. So, my position was secured very close to the face of the person reading the names.

Names were read on and on. The process went on for several hours without anyone acknowledging the names read so far. Being at the edge of the table, I could scan each page of the list as soon as the clerk opened it, before the reading of that page started. When my name was not on the list, I would pray silently so that no one else in the audience would be on that page. The process had started around 9a.m. It must have been around 1p.m. when the first name from the audience was found. The first successful name found was Francis Egbuniwe.

So, one position out of three was gone. I had only two more chances of entering Saint Finbarr's College. I intensified my silent prayers. But instead of being picked second, someone else was picked to fill the next open position. The second successful name found was Joseph Molokwu.

After what seemed like more endless hours, I spotted my name about the middle of a newly opened page. I screamed, "That's my name, that's my name, on this page, that's my name." "My name is here!," sticking my finger at my name listed on the page. This unauthorized announcement caught everyone off guard. I was shouted at to keep quiet. Names must be read from the top to the bottom. There would be no interjection to the middle of the page. When the clerk got to that point, the name would be called. So, I kept quiet as chided. I further intensified my silent prayers. "God, let no one else be called ahead of my name on that page." I am sure that the Good Lord was listening to my juvenile prayers. The third, and final successful name found was Bodunde Badiru.

Although the passage of time has eroded my recollection of the exact events of that day, the agony of the tense waiting has remained etched in my memory. In later years at the school, Francis, Joseph, and I, along with Joseph's close friend, Michael Elumeze, would engage in endless debates as to who was picked first, second, or third. I still feel the torment of waiting to be picked third. So, I remember the order clearly. Father Slattery came back onto the scene to formalize the selection of the three kids. He announced that these three kids were the new students of Saint Finbarr's College.

1. Francis Egbuniwe (now late)
2. Joseph Molokwu
3. Bodunde Badiru

They must show up to start classes in the morning, without delay. School had already started two weeks earlier. So, we must start attending classes forthwith.

Thus, I began my secondary school education at Saint Finbarr's College in January 1968. Father Slattery handled the admission process his own way. It was fair, just, and transparent. It was right there in the open field. No flattery, no pretensions. There were no private meetings. There were no under-the-table deals. It was the only way I could have entered a reputable secondary school in 1968. All other doors had been slammed shut. Father Slattery opened the door of educational opportunity for me, without consideration of age, color, creed, race, tribe, language, financial status, political leaning, or religious affiliation. It was totally on the basis of merit. He let the best in the pool of prospective students rise to the top to claim the three prized positions. Can you see my point now? It was a special blessing for me. I hope readers can now understand why writing this book (the third in a series) is very special for me. I cannot imagine going to my grave without committing this story to a published book. I am extraordinarily indebted to Father Slattery. Writing this book is the only way I can reward his kindness and fairness. Leaders of today and tomorrow should learn a lot from Father Slattery's ways. A class photo for my 1970 Class IIIA is shown in Figure 20. Those in the photo are identified as follow:

Figure 20. Finbarr's 1970 Class IIIA Group Photo

Front row (kneeling) left to right:
Richard Egbaiyelo, Sodunke Babajide, Oluwole Cole, Michael Elumeze, Benedict Ikwenobe, Abimbola Aibinu, Ernest Ndiwe, Femi Dos Reis

Second row- left to right:
Mr. A. A. Kpotie (Biology Teacher), Joseph Obasa, Charles Hazoume, Ekong Udoffia (late), Wale Adewoyin, Francis Egbuniwe (late), Olayinka Sanni (late), Bodunde Badiru, Babatunde Ogunde, Ayodele Omokoya, Jonathan

Egboh (late), Femi Olanrewaju (late), Joseph Molokwu, Visiting teacher from NCE (National College of Education)

Back row- left to right:
Emmanuel Nwaise, Joseph Olisemeka, Pius Danso, Emmanuel Ohikere, Anthony Edem, Adetola Alimi, Adegboyega Solarin, Felix Membu (late), Layiwola Ladenegan, Onofiok Ufot, Philip Bieni, Babatunde Akinwunmi, Akinsola Akinsete (snr).

A much-cherished photo taken in our physics lab in 1970 is shown in Figure 21. Those appearing in the photo are Egbaiyelo, Bodunde Badiru, Membu, late Francis Egbuniwe, Ayodele Omokoya, and late Olayinka Sanni.

Figure 21. Finbarr's 1970 Physics Lab Photo

Chapter Three

Discipline at Saint Finbarr's College

Discipline was (and still is) a major attribute and attraction of Saint Finbarr's College. Parents take delight in the discipline that kids get at the school. The mantra of the school revolves around three tenets of:

1. Academics
2. Sports
3. Discipline

The school was widely noted and respected for these desirable attributes. Father Slattery provided the educational infrastructure to pursue academics. He also provided the sports environment to ensure the accomplishment of an esteemed football prowess. Finally, he was personally present and involved in meting out discipline whenever needed by any unruly student. He was a no-nonsense school principal. Although he was a man of small stature, his physical presence was threatening enough to debar students for unauthorized acts. He often carried a stick (not a real cane), which he threatened to wield and apply to straighten out behaviors. No one dared confront him. He boasted he could box and beat any boy that challenged his authority. No one dared. Mostly, the boys just laughed in admiration of his ways. A common warning Call around the school was "Father is coming, Father is coming," the response to which would send congregating boys scurrying back to where they were supposed to be. Father Slattery roamed the campus intermittently and unannounced in his attempt to catch boys in the act of being unruly or out of place. There was a rule for everything. Abiding by those rules helped in shaping the future outlook of the students.

The disciplinary framework of the school permanently shaped the attitude of students in how they apply themselves, not only to their studies, but also to every endeavor outside the school, in the community, and in future career pursuits. He would say, "Apply whatever skills you've got to whatever you are required to tackle." In this light, cartoon experiments that I engaged in while practicing in the art room of Saint Finbarr's College led to a brief opportunity to draw cartoon strips for the children's page of the Daily Times in 1970 and 1971. The art teacher and Father Slattery were very proud of this "educational outreach" as they called it because I had a contract and got paid for the cartoons that were published in the newspaper in a special children's column called "Fun with BB." BB, acronym for Bodunde Badiru, was my popular nickname at Saint Finbarr's College. Many of my classmates and neighborhood childhood friends still call me BB to this date. The Daily Times cartoon column was a big accomplishment for a high school kid in those days. My first payment voucher from The Daily Times of Nigeria, dated July 10, 1972, was for one British Pound and One Shilling (£1: 1s). Nowadays, that would be about $1.20 at today's conversion rate. In 1972, that was a hefty pay for a high school kid and it was my first ever income for services provided. Father Slattery was particularly impressed because the school was still relatively young and needed to build a good reputation in other areas apart from football. So, he would widely commend and publicize any outside accomplishments to other students of the school during the morning assembly.

As a part of my personal demonstration of self-discipline, during my attendance at Finbarr's, I occasionally resided with my sister at the Unilag Staff Quarters. Whenever she did not have a house help, I would move in with her to provide household support covering all manners of household chores including kitchen service and gardening. My present affinity for the kitchen and household chores was shaped in those years. Living so close to the college often created temptations for us to sneak out of school during school hours. This was a no-no according to the rules of the school. But young boys always enjoy the challenge (and perils) of doing what they are told not to do. If we managed to sneak out without being caught by Father Slattery, we would visit the homes of classmates living at Akoka and make the long trek to Lagoon at the edge of Unilag campus – in search of fun and play. Thinking back now, it was a big risk. I can never explain why we would have risked being permanently expelled from the school. Whenever we successfully got out and back to the school compound, we would feel a sense of great accomplishment. With that euphoria, we would start looking forward to the next opportunity to sneak out again. I thank God that no one in my group of friends was ever caught engaging in this mischievous act. Boys that were caught faced the full wrath of Father Slattery. I did my best to stay out of such wrath. In fact, I earned a good Testimonial from Father Slattery when I graduated. He was never bashful to write straight testimonials, whether good or bad. He signed every document directly by himself. Original documents signed by Father Slattery are highly-priced documents by those who had the good fortune to have received a signed document from him.

A December 1998 Christmas Card from Father Slattery to the Badiru Family contains his usual statements of blessings. The card remains a cherished item in the family's collection of memorable items. The greetings, in Father Slattery's own aged handwriting, reads as follows:

"Dear Adedeji B. Badiru
Congratulations for all the letters from U.S. and also thank you for the Video. Received it here in Ireland on Twenty-third November 1998.
I hope a member of my family will tape it and send a copy to our Boss – Blackock Road, Cork. It will be kept in the Archives and probably used occasionally to help the cause of the Mission.
I was very proud of all the old boys who appeared on the Video. Your speeches were wonderful. You made it a historic and unique occasion.
You will be happy to know that I am all set for my return journey to Lagos – I hope to continue for some time the work of the Mission and pay a special attention to Finbarr's and the old boys and the new.
Thanks for all you have done for the Alma Mater.
Greet your wife and children. May God Bless you all.
Happy and holy Christmas.
God bless you.
Denis Slattery"

Recalling the discipline impacted by my years at Saint Finbarr's College, I created what I called the equation of success for my students. The axiom, referred to as "Badiru's Equations of Success," entreats students to rely more on their self-discipline in accomplishing goals and objectives. The equation says that success is a function of three primary factors: raw intelligence, common sense, and self-discipline.

Success = f(Intelligence, Common Sense, Self-discipline)

Intelligence is an innate attribute, which every one of us is endowed with. Common sense is an acquired trait from our everyday social interactions. Self-Discipline is an inner drive (personal control), which helps an individual to blend common sense with intelligence in order to achieve success.

With this equation, success is within everyone's control. One cannot succeed on intelligence alone. Common sense and self-discipline must be used to facilitate success.

The tremendous discipline of accomplishments of Father Slattery can even be assessed based on my art classroom experience of those days, where we had abundant supply of water to clean our paint brushes after each miscue of a paint hue. Nowadays, such abundance of water supply is non-existent in many academic institutions. Water is rationed to the extent that unintended color tones enter into classroom artistic experiments. With the abundance of educational resources, we had no excuse for not demonstrating discipline in the pursuit of our academic subjects at Saint Finbarr's College.

Chapter Four

Sports at Saint Finbarr's College

Sports is essential for human interaction and development. The absence of it can be demoralizing, as was seen during the worldwide COVID-19 pandemic. Father Slattery, earlier on, recognized the connection between sports and the development of the complete student. Thus, he ensured that all students (during his time at the school) were exposed to diverse opportunities to participate in sports or sports appreciation. Academics was required of all students. Discipline was demanded of all students. Sports was encouraged for all students. His philosophy was "try it, you may be good at it and you may like it." Apart from the highly-regarded school-level teams, sports participation at Saint Finbarr's College was readily available through a variety of inter-house sports competition. Even I, without the physique of a sports star, still got to participate at the unadorned levels of Finbarr's sports. I participated in inter-house tracks and in the developmental soccer teams, sarcastically referred to as the "mosquito team" and "rabbit team." These were the junior level teams designed to prepare boys for the full-fledged first-eleven team later on. My self-proclaimed nickname for playing soccer was "Iron Pillar." Some of my fun-loving classmates (notably Benedict Ikwenobe) translated the nickname into different variations. These invoked a lot of fun and laughter whenever we were on a playing field. Although I was a decent player, I was never committed to being on the regular team of Saint Finbarr's College. Late Mr. Anthony Omoera (former principal), while coaching our rabbit team, lamented that if I would fully commit to playing soccer, I could be a superb Finbarr's player. Of course, the competition for securing a spot on the regular team was incredibly keen and I wasn't fully committed to training to be a regular soccer player. I focused more on the academics and discipline pillars of Finbarr's. Saint Finbarr's College soccer players were of a different stock – highly skilled and talented. Many of them, even in high school, could have played on professional teams. In fact, the 1970 team was so good that there was a plan to have the team play the professional team Stationery Stores. But the untimely death of Chief Israel Adebajo, the owner of Stationery Stores, just one day before the scheduled match, scuttled the plan. So, we never got to find out if our high school team could have beaten a full-fledged professional team. In my later years, recalling my Saint Finbarr's soccer heritage, I did blossom into a more respectable recreational player. I played on my university soccer team at Tennessee Technological University and later on adult recreational teams in Florida and Oklahoma.

True to my Finbarr's soccer pedigree, I organized a neighborhood soccer team at Ebute Metta, named Afro-Melody Football Club. I organize, managed, and coached the rag-tag team. My membership card for the team is shown in Figure 22.

Figure 22. Soccer Club ID Card

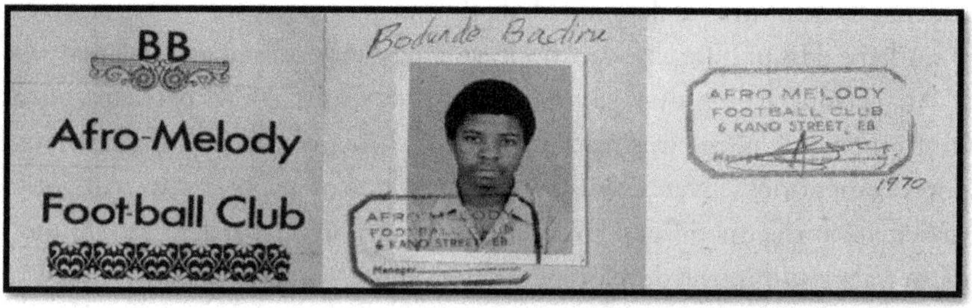

An interesting letter from one competing team, named Star Light Football Club, is reproduced below:

From:
STAR LIGHT FOOTBALL
102, Freeman Street

Ebute-Metta
14th August 1973

To:
The Secretary
Afro-Melody Football Club
6 Kano Street
Ebute-Metta

Dear Sir,

RETURN MATCH

We shall be pleased, if you could please, arrange to have a Return Match of the Football played at the Railway Institute, which ended in a 3-0 defeat in your favor on Sunday, 19th August, 1973 at LOCO RAILWAY FOOTBALL GROUND, YABA.

Kick Off   8:30a.m.

Looking forward to receiving your acceptance in due course while wishing your club more progress.

Yours in Sport,

Signed, Secretary

This letter is refreshing for many reasons. First, it demonstrates the continuation of the promotion of sports commitment as of 1973, after I had left Finbarr's. Second, it shows how self-organized we were with amateur sports engagements at our young ages of between 18 and 23 years old. Third, it confirms the formality we affiliated with our sports pursuits, via the use of formal written letters. Fourth, the 3-0 victory proves that my team was, indeed, good, in the true spirit and expectation of Finbarr's.

I was also was an Ad-Hoc organizer and coach of our impromptu Form V-A Team at Saint Finbarr's College. In my research for writing this book, one document that I uncovered in my archive of Finbarr's files is a soccer game lineup that I drew up for a match on June 6, 1972. The lineup had Reis in goal, Egbaiyelo in full back, Sanni, Omokoya, and Elumeze as half-backs, Ikwe and Femi as mid-fielders, and Alimi, Sholarin, Membu, and Badiru as forwards. The hand-drawn lineup carried the original approval signature of Father Slattery. The signature signifies how Father Slattery held a tight rein on all organized activities at the school. Continuing the sports tradition, in later years, I organized and coached adult soccer teams in Norman, Oklahoma (USA). I was a coach and player. The team, named The Crusaders, won several local soccer championships. The soccer-success exploits of the team were documented in detail in my first book on The Physics of Soccer, published in 2010. I also briefly coached my younger son's youth soccer teams in Oklahoma and Tennessee. My soccer affinity (thanks to Finbarr's) led me to the development of my popular soccer website, www.PhysicsofSoccer.com.

Inter-house sports were another big part of the experience at Saint Finbarr's College. Although I participated in several sports at the school, I was always only on the fringes of excellence in each one. My primary goal was more to be a part of the fun of sports. I don't recall devoting the necessary training time needed to excel. But I occasionally used the pretext of going for sports training at the school to escape from home so that I could go and play elsewhere. My sister always gave me permission to go out if I connected the reason to some sports activity at the school. She knew sports was very important at Saint Finbarr's and she never wanted to interfere with the school's expectations.

Father Slattery, being a Games Master and an International Referee, was very eager to put the school at the forefront quickly in football since it would take 5 years for the school to prove its excellence in academics. In its first year of existence, it pitched itself in a football match against its host Primary School, St. Paul's Primary School, Apapa Road and lost 1-2. In 1957, it faced much older St. Gregory's "Rabbits," where Father Slattery himself had been a Games Master. The school later had a number of matches with another older School, the Ahmadiya College, Agege. It was a very ambitious venture for the school, in its first four years of existence on 3rd June 1960, to make its first attempt on the Zard Cup, a nationwide inter-Secondary School competition, which later became the Principals Cup. The school again lost to its counterpart institution, St. Gregory's College, 1-3. In 1961 it met the school again and lost 0-1 after an initial draw of 2-2. In 1962, Saint Finbarr's College won the

Principals Cup for the first time, only six years after being established. This victory was repeated in 1966, 1968, and 1969. From then the team from Saint Finbarr's College became the team to beat. Weaker teams feared any match with Saint Finbarr's while stronger ones like C.M.S. Grammar School, Baptist Academy, Igbobi College, and of course, the big brother Saint Gregory's College, always looked forward to a tough encounter. In 1971, 1972, and 1973, the school kept the Principals Cup, having won it three consecutive times.

It is noteworthy that in the 1970's and 1980's the school produced international players like Thompson Oliha, Nduka Ugbade, Samson SiaSia, and Henry Nwosu, just to mention a few. In fact, in those days, for any candidate to aspire to come to St. Finbarr's, he had to be academically sound and/or physically superior in football. Stephen Keshi, who captained a Finbarr's team, went on to captain and coach national teams. In an era when some holy men are charged with doing unholy things, Father Slattery was holy and dedicated to the cause throughout his life of sanctity. There was no flattery or fakery about him.

"Slattery, No Flattery" was a common catchphrase in Lagos, Nigeria about the ways and deeds of Father Slattery. A picture is worth a thousand words. There are not enough words to describe the immense widespread contributions of Reverend Denis Joseph Slattery to education in Nigeria. Even after his death since 2003, his deeds continue to influence the lives of those who ever had the good fortune to be associated with Father Slattery either directly or through the continuing legacy of his Saint Finbarr's College, Akoka-Yaba, Lagos, Nigeria.

In the days of Father Slattery, all roads led to Saint Finbarr's College, Akoka, Yaba. All parents in Lagos wished and clamored for their children to go to Saint Finbarr's College, even though there were several other highly-regarded secondary schools in Lagos, including King's College, Igbobi College, Saint Gregory's College, Ansa-ud-deen College, Baptist Academy, and so on. As a high school aspirant in those days, my own initial goal was to attend King's College, until I came across the educational and sports triumphs of Saint Finbarr's College and the personal and direct touch of Father Slattery. It was a dichotomy of a special kind to have a school that excelled in sports (football, i.e., soccer) while simultaneously winning national accolades in educational accomplishments. I was provisionally selected for an interview to enter King's College, but I was utterly devastated when I did not make the cut. By divine intervention, Saint Finbarr's College came along and I was admitted. I was elated. The story of my admission to Saint Finbarr's College is still a fortuitous occurrence that still astonishes me even today. Had I not gained a last-minute admission to Saint Finbarr's during that 1968 admission cycle, it would have been an up-hill challenge, if not an impossible pursuit, during the next annual admissions cycle. I am convinced today that I would not have been any more competitive in 1969 than I was in 1968 in entering a reputable high school in Lagos area. The positive experience of how Saint Finbarr's College came to my academic rescue still determines how I view educational opportunities these days and how I fervently support giving educational opportunities to qualified young minds of today.

Reverend Father Joseph Slattery was born in Fermoy in the County of Cork, South Ireland, on 29th February, 1916, a product of a strong Irish heritage. The Irish are noted for their constant search for self-determination among dominant neighbors. He later became a Catholic priest, founder of Schools, sport administrator, an editor, and a journalist. Father Slattery is a leap-year child. He was always very proud of his leap-year birth date, claiming to be only one-fourth of his actual age. His parents, Mr. Timothy Slattery and Mrs. Kate Slattery (Née Curtin), were blessed with eight children. Denis was the seventh child of the family. Timothy Slattery was a master-cutter and Kate Slattery was a trained dress-maker. They were both from Barrington, Fermoy, a little provincial town in the County of Cork, in the south of Ireland, where the Slattery generations had lived since the 13th century.

The Slattery family was known as "Doers"; a family with a deep sense of adventure, enterprise, and great achievement. The Irish adventurous spirit has remained their greatest contribution to the world. They stride the world in pastoral and political life, breaking new grounds in all spheres.

The American people today remember the Irish among them as the descendants of the builders of Modern America. In 1776, at the signing of the American Constitution, six Irish citizens were signatories to that historic instrument of governance. Timothy Slattery was a disciplinarian, stern, and straight. Kate Slattery was a quiet, serene, and very charitable lady – a combination that was perhaps very necessary for raising eight children, six boys and two girls.

The Slatterys were a family of sportsmen, a trait presumably taken from their father. Timothy Slattery was a great footballer and represented his country as a potential sportsman. His children, particularly Denis, simply carried on the tradition. At a very tender age, Denis Slattery was enrolled for his kindergarten education at the Christian Brothers School in Fermoy. He was the only Slattery who did not attend the local Convent school. Young Denis refused to go "to the nuns" at the Presentation Convent. At the Christian Brothers School, the young Slattery was remembered as a wild young man. A healthy kind of wildness, they would say. His activities included *"climbing the highest tree over the River Blackwater and plunging into the deepest depth, searching the woods and forest for birds' nests and eggs, and following the grey hounds on Sunday Soccer."*

He became an Altar boy at the age of ten. He was an excellent liturgist but an average Altar boy. Once an old man who was regular at Mass called him and said, "You serve Mass beautifully. I think you will make a priest." This seemingly harmless remark would come to plant the seed of his vocation. Young Denis had a seriousness of purpose and had often talked about vocations and in due time, he entered the Junior Secondary.

In the Seminary, life was rather drab and hard. Food was poor, dormitories were badly heated, and the chapel was only heated on Sundays. By the second year he had sciatica. He recovered and buried himself deeper into his chosen vocation. He spent two years in the seminary. The extra year was spent getting private tuition in Latin to enable him to pass the Matriculation examination.

The year 1932 marked when Denis Joseph Slattery began his missionary vocation. By 1934, he entered the Novitiate in Clough for a period of two years, and on the 17th December, 1939, he was ordained a priest. He was studious and prayerful at the major Seminary, so he was chosen to go to Rome and study the scriptures in 1940. He was not destined to be in Rome! The 2nd World War broke out and Mussolini shook hands with Hitler, so Rome was out for young Father Denis.

Reverend Father Slattery's first assignment after ordainment was to contribute to raising money for the Church. He felt humiliated because he had to practically beg. Little did he realize that he would be doing the same for the rest of his life. This was the beginning of an arduous and tasking pastoral life.

In faraway Lagos, Nigeria, Archbishop Leo Taylor was in dire need of teachers for his diocese. In 1941, the 2nd World War was at its peak. Reverend Father Denis Joseph Slattery, 25-year-old Catholic Priest of the Society of African Missions (SMA), was on his way to his posting in Africa. This young Irish priest was part of a growing Irish spiritual empire that included China and the Philippines. The trip was punctuated by a German air attack on the convoy. A German plane had dropped 3 bombs on their ship, which was sailing from Glasgow in a convoy of 50 ships carrying Allied Forces on the Atlantic Ocean. In the tremor following the bombing, the ship rocked violently, dipping from left to right, but did not sink. When they finally sailed into Lagos, the Germans were presumably bombing the Lagos port and ships were not berthing. The ship headed for Port-Harcourt where she berthed. The journey was continued by train from Port-Harcourt to Kaduna to Lagos.

Lagos in 1941 had its fascination for the young Irishman. This is the white man's grave, he wondered. But he did not reckon with Ilawe-Ekiti, a little village in the hinterland of the Western part of Nigeria. Archbishop Taylor was waiting in Lagos. He would welcome the young priest and send him to Ilawe-Ekiti. On his first night at Ilawe-Ekiti, young Father Slattery was confronted by a strange pastoral duty. At midnight, a black face had poked its head into the house to ask the Reverend Father to come immediately and give blessing to a dying Christian. He performed his pastoral duties, but the picture remained with him; the black face and the black night.

By the 1940s Archbishop Leo Taylor had built a strong missionary base in the Lagos Diocese. Well-respected and loved by many, Archbishop Taylor was a member of the Society of African Missions (SMA) and of course, the quintessential missionary. He was to recall Reverend Father Slattery to Lagos in 1942. By now the young priest he sent to Ilawe-Ekiti now spoke the Yoruba language and could give confession in the language. In Lagos, he was posted to St. Gregory's College, Obalende, as a teacher and games master. His stature seemed to have endeared him to his new students. A mutual relationship was formed which led to great exploits in the football field. The stay at St. Gregory's College was short.

In 1943, he was posted to the Catholic Printing Press as journalist and later Editor of *Catholic Herald*. At the Herald he cultivated a radical posture and became concerned about Nigeria's self-determination as he thundered from the newspaper and the pulpit, "Nigeria for Nigerians." His years as Editor of the Catholic Herald were turbulent. Through the paper, he contributed to the pre-independence struggle, forming a lasting relationship with Labour leaders and politicians. He used the Herald to champion the workers' cause during the general strike of 1945 and the Enugu Coal Mine strike where twenty striking miners were killed. Thrice, the British Colonial Government tried to throw him out of the country, after several warnings. But according to him he was just doing his duty. *"The British are gone and I (Slattery) am still here,"* Slattery would later boast. Father Slattery later went on to write his Masters thesis on the labour struggle in Nigeria. A founding member of the Nigerian Union of Journalists (NUJ) and the Guild of Editors, Father Slattery contributed immensely to labour and journalism.

Also during these years, he made remarkable contributions to the development of football and football administration in Nigeria. As an inside-left, he had played first division football in Lagos with the Lagos United. But it was as a referee that he made his greatest contribution. His Excellency, Nnamdi Azikiwe, first President of the Federal Republic of Nigeria, was Slattery's linesman in those days. He recalls that he made great strides as a referee probably because he was a Catholic priest; therefore, he was presumed honest. Reverend Father Denis Slattery was, at different times, the Chairman of the Referees' Association, Executive member of the Lagos Amateur Football Association, and Chairman of the Nigerian Football Association (N.F.A.)

In 1956, Archbishop Taylor invited Father Denis Slattery to establish a secondary school in Lagos. Father Slattery saw this assignment as an opportunity to contribute to society as an educationist and a sports administrator. Thus, in January, 1956, he founded St. Finbarr's College as a Technical Grammar School. Classes started on the premises of St. Paul's Primary School, Ebute Metta. St. Finbarr's College became the first school in Nigeria to run in duality a Technical and Grammar School. This was an educational innovation that endeared the school to parents. Father Slattery chose to name the school after Saint Finbarr, who was a great educator, a priest, and a bishop who founded a monastery of prayer and an institution.

In 1960, the school was approved by the Ministry of Education. By this singular action St. Finbarr's College became eligible to participate in the prestigious schoolboys' football competition, the Principal Cup. This had a special thrill for Reverend Father Slattery. He had one burning ambition since the day he founded St. Finbarr's College – to win the prestigious Principal Cup! The name, St. Finbarr's College, was to become synonymous with schoolboy soccer and academic excellence in Nigeria.

Having moved from the premises of St. Paul's Primary School, Ebute Metta to its permanent site in Akoka in 1959, St. Finbarr's College made its debut in the Principal Cup in 1960. They lost to St. Gregory's College that year and in 1961. But in 1962, St. Finbarr's College won the Principal Cup. This was the beginning of unprecedented soccer supremacy in schoolboy football. The college went on to win the Principal Cup for a record nine times. The secret of this success was physical fitness, the provision of necessary training equipment, and a standard pitch (playing field). The myth goes to say that had Father Slattery coached the Nigerian national side of those days, they would have won the World Cup. Today, some of his concepts on football administration still remain valid.

Football was the delight of the students of St. Finbarr's; still, Father Slattery succeeded in pushing for excellence in other sporting endeavours. In 1960, the College made her debut in the Grier Cup. That year, Eddy Akika of St. Finbarr's College took the coveted Victor Ludorum Trophy winning the Hurdles, Long Jump, and second in the High Jump event.

Slattery ensured that sporting excellence was clearly tied to academic excellence. Through the years and on many occasions, the College had the enviable record of scoring a 100% pass in the WAEC entries. Thus, students of St. Finbarr's were noted for hard work and hard play. Today, Saint Finbarr's College has produced numerous Nigerians who got to the peak of their professional careers and contributed significantly to the development of the Nation. Notable amongst them are: Vice-Admiral Patrick Koshoni (Retired), Major-General Cyril Iweze, Nze Mark Odu, Otunba Anthony Olusegun Odugbesan, Dr. J. A. Ikem, Dr. Segun Ogundimu, Chief Empire Kanu P, Professor Steve Elesha, Dr. Tayo Shokunbi, Airvice Marshal Wilfred Ozah, Tom Borha, Segun Ajanlekoko.

Father Denis Slattery retired from St. Finbarr's College in 1975. He returned to his first love, his pastoral duties. So, to St. Denis Catholic Church, Bariga he retired; to a total service to the Church as Parish priest. He eventually retired as Vicar-General to the Archdiocese of Lagos, and left his footprints again, in the sand of time. Father Slattery was a true Nigerian patriot of Irish parentage, who contributed to the pioneering of technical education in secondary schools and the growth of football administration in Nigeria. Father Slattery was a Missionary, Educationist, Journalist, Technocrat, Football Administrator, a mentor of sports, and one of nature's exceptional gentlemen.

Reverend Father Slattery was an outstanding example of the Irish Catholic Missionary movement, which in this century saw many thousands of Irish Reverend Fathers and Sisters leave Ireland to take the Christian message to the four corners of the world. He dedicated 56 years of his earthly life to the development of the Nigerian humanity. A keen sportsman and Journalist, he served Nigeria in many capacities including Chairmanship of the Nigerian Football Association (NFA). He also edited the Catholic Herald Newspaper for many years. He brought with him from Ireland, a keen appreciation of the value of education, without which freedom, responsibility, or development is impossible. In his great desire to inform, Father Slattery became actively involved in the development of Journalism and Education. His major contribution to education, St. Finbarr's College, Akoka, is named after Saint Finbarr – the patron saint of his native county of Cork. His other enduring legacy to Nigeria, football, comes from his own passionate love of sport. Here, he obviously tapped into a rich vein in Nigerian life – a truly fanatical love of football. A list of his achievements and contributions is presented below.

Slattery's Achievements and Contributions

1. Vice-Chairman of the Society for the Bribe Scorners
2. Assistant Honorary Secretary of the Nigerian Olympic & British Empire Games Association
3. Publicity Secretary of the Lagos District Amateur Football Association
4. Member of the Council of African Students in North America
5. Assistant Secretary of the Nigerian Football Association
6. Honorary Secretary of the Commonwealth Games Appeal Fund
7. Catholic Representative of the Broadcasting Services (Religious)
8. Chairman of the Nigerian Referees Association

9. Chairman of the Council of Social Workers (Boy Scouts, Catholic Youth Organization, Salvation Army, Boys' Brigade, Y.M.C.A., Colony Welfare Organizations, Girls Guide, and Youth Clubs)
10. Chairman of the Leper Colony of Nigeria
11. Chairman of the Nigerian Football Association (NFA)
12. Editor of the Catholic Herald (Newspaper)
13. Foundation Member of the Nigerian Union of Journalists
14. Member of the Nigerian Guild of Editors
15. Founder and Principal of St. Finbarr's College, Akoka, Lagos
16. Founder of SS Peter & Paul, Shomolu
17. Founder of Our Lady of Fatima Private School, Bariga
18. Founder of St. Joseph's Vocational School, Akoka
19. Coordinator of the T.I.M.E. Project, Akoka
20. Founder of St. Finbarr's Catholic Church, Akoka, Lagos
21. Founder of St. Gabriel's Catholic Church
22. Founder of St. Flavius Catholic Church, Oworonshoki
23. Parish Priest of St. Denis Catholic Church
24. Vicar-General of the Catholic Church of Nigeria – Lagos Archdiocese (Retired)

My personal recollections of some favorite passages from Father Slattery's book (Slattery, 1996) are echoed in the paragraphs that follow.

Before his death, SFCOBA beseeched Father Slattery to give us his own account of the recollection of Saint Finbarr's College in the early days. Below is what he told us:

"The Queen of England visited Nigeria during one of those years. When I bowed and shook hands with the Queen, I was quickly passed on to the Duke. The Queen took much more notice of the ladies in the line. Apparently, the Duke knew about my association with Football and refereeing. In the short conversation we had he made a very profound statement that I often used afterwards with an air of pride. The Duke of Edinburgh said to me, "Football is as good as its referee. A bad referee can spoil Soccer."

"But what has happened to our beloved country, one of the richest gems of Africa? What has become of all our dreams? How many have paid the supreme price

sacrificing their lives at home and in foreign lands to build a new Nigeria? Literally thousands died in Egypt, North Africa, Burma, etc.

Look at Nigeria today, several years after independence. Today, sad to say, Nigeria is riddled with corruption from the top to the bottom. No segment of Nigerian Society is free from the Cankerworm of bribery that has eaten into the bowels of our nation."

"As a result of a lecture I gave one time when I blamed the budding political leaders that they had fallen very quickly for the flesh pots offered by the Colonialists by taking huge salaries as ministers with or without portfolios, (I stated that there was no Freedom in Nigeria but our neo-political leaders were dancing to the tune of the British overlords), the next day, I was on the receiving end of a few scathing remarks in the press.

One paper wrote, "Father Slattery must have been drugged or drunk. He could not see wood or the trees!!

But another paper replied, "Father Slattery is destined to be the 'Cardinal Minzenty' of Hungary to be sacrificed on the altar of British imperialism." I was neither. I was Catholic Priest that stood for freedom – freedom to worship the true God and to enjoy the good things of life."

"I always regarded the visit to the Holy Land as a gift from my people in Nigeria. Had I not come to Nigeria in the first place, I probably would not have ever visited those sacred places that are particularly dear to the Catholic Priest.

Thank you Nigeria for this wonderful gift on my 11th birthday, when I turned 44 years old. Don't forget that I am a Leap Year Child."

The Four Commandments of St. Finbarr's In Slattery's Time

Actually, there were "Four Commandments", not ten, strictly implemented to help maintain discipline. Any student violating these rules went down that "Corridor of no return." This had become a catch phrase in the school. These were the commandments:

Any student caught stealing will be expelled.

Any student caught copying at examination time will be expelled. Any student that fails is automatically expelled. He is not allowed to Repeat.

Any student leaving the compound during school hours without the Principal's permission will be expelled.

Any student caught smoking or with drugs will be expelled.

These were often discussed as the moral pillars of St. Finbarr's College, and the key to our policy. Proved beyond a shadow of doubt after thorough investigation, there was no mercy shown, even to a Form 1 Boy if caught breaking these decrees."

Slattery, No Lottery

Everything about Father Slattery was for real and no lottery. He never sought fame and accolades. His approach was based on resolute pursuit rather than a game-of-chance undertaking. He pursued and did everything with resolute and unwavering commitment. He called each thing as he saw it. He was not a man of narrative pontification. He got to the point and that was it. Period.

To further appreciate my story, the reader must understand the background of Reverend Father Denis Joseph Slattery, the Irish priest who touched the lives of many Nigerians. He was an exceptional human being from the time he was born on 29th February, 1916 until his death on 10th July, 2003.

In a 1996 newspaper editorial, the writer Ochereome Nnanna presented an accurate characterization of Father Slattery on his eightieth birthday as a man of no flattery. A true renaissance man, Father Slattery said it as he saw it. All the accolades that Father Slattery has received over the years, both while he was alive and following his death, contain the same unmistakable fact. There was never any flattery about him. He was a man of no pretensions. What you saw was what you got from him. I have tried to pattern myself after him in that regard. A friend once called me "Deji of no pretensions." I still cherish that characterization.

Father Slattery prided himself as an Irish-Nigerian and has been credited with many contributions to the development of modern Nigeria (both pre-independence and following independence). He was a patriot to the core, an activist for righteousness not only from the standpoint of religion, but also from the points of social equality and political self-determination. His 1996 Memoirs, *My Life Story*, published by West African Book Publishers, Ltd. gives a very detailed account of his contributions to Nigeria and Nigerians.

One admirable attribute of his work in Nigeria was his commitment to a non-parochial view of issues. He supported the views of different religious leanings, as long as the views matched the tenets of good citizenship. There was religious tolerance at St. Finbarr's College. There was tolerance of every economic status. Similarly, there was complete tribal and ethnic harmony at the school because Father Slattery saw to it that everyone accepted everyone else.

As Principal of Saint Finbarr's College from 1956 through 1975, Father Slattery used the threat of being expelled as a deterrent to discourage bad behavior by students. His common warning was "I will send you down that dirt road, and you will never come back, and God is my witness" He, of course, was referring to a one-way journey down the narrow dirt road of Akoka. Saint Finbarr's College campus was the one building in that area of Akoka at that time. It was a long dusty hike from the Unilag Road to the school with heavy bushes on either side of the road.

Father Slattery was a man of small stature. But his heart, energy, and enthusiasm matched those of a giant. He put his energetic temperament into good use in chasing misbehaving students around the school compound. With his robe flowing wildly in the wind, he would take off after boys that he suspected were contravening school rules. It was almost a game of cat and mouse. He monitored the school premises himself. Latecomers and those sneaking out of the school compound during the day hardly escaped his roving eyes. He could run. He could jump. He could even tackle ruffian boys and oh yes, he could really shout. He was a multi-faceted principal; and we all admired, revered, and feared him all at the same time. He also prided himself on being a boxer. Whether he was actually ever a boxer, or whether he put on that bluff to keep us in line, was a frequent debate among the students. When angered, he would challenge the students to a fistfight. Of course, he knew none of us would dare take him on, and he capitalized on that fact. Secondary school kids were much bigger in those days. We had classmates who were in their early twenties. Yet, none was big or man enough to confront the wrath of Father Slattery.

"Father is coming" was a frequently look-out call from boys doing what they were not supposed to be doing. Just like prairie dogs scenting an approaching predator, the boys would run helter-skelter in different directions. There would often be one unfortunate (slower) boy that would be chased down by Father. He would drag the boy into the principal's office for an appropriate punishment. At the next school assembly, we would all hear about the latest mischievous acts of "a few bad boys." I think Father Slattery probably enjoyed those encounters as a way to get his exercise in order to keep fit and trim. He was a nurturing disciplinarian. As strict as he was as a disciplinarian, Father Slattery was also a very forgiving individual. One minute he was shouting and ranting about something, the next minute he was patting you on the back for a good academic or football performance.

How he found the time, resolve, and energy to do all that he did was beyond explanation. Those of us who have tried to emulate his ways can usually be identified by our diverse interests both in avocation and recreation. Father Slattery was a very effervescent man; always excited and animated about everything. There was never a dull moment with him around.

After all these years, Saint Finbarr's College continues to excel in Academics, Sports, and Discipline. As of the time of this writing (2018), the school continues to receive accolades for its multi-dimensional accomplishments. In 2017, Business Day Research and Intelligence Unit (BRIU) published a guide to the best schools in Lagos, Nigeria. Saint Finbarr's College was listed among the topmost secondary schools in Lagos State. The school's performance in the West African Senior School Certificate Examinations since 2013 have been extraordinary. Based on the number of students who obtained five credits including Mathematics and English Language, the pass rates have been 98.7% in 2013, 100% in 2014, 97.4% in 2015 95%, in 2016 97.4% and 98.2% in 2017. Finbarr's students have been winning laurels at various academic competitions, including Helmbridge, Olympiad, Inter-collegiate Quiz and Debate, and so on.

Please score a checkmark for academics!

In the same vein, Saint Finbarr's College won Soccer Guarantee Trust (GT) Bank Championship on June 29, 2017 at Onikan Stadium, Lagos, Nigeria. The school has expanded its sports excellence to include basketball, tennis, volleyball and, badminton.

Please score a checkmark for sports excellence!

Overall, the virtues of discipline, self-control, respect, care for others, honesty, obedience, hard work, dedication, diligence, and resilience continue to be instilled in Finbarr's students on a daily basis. Thus, Saint Finbarr's College provides holistic education for its students.

Chapter 4 References

1. Slattery, Denis J (1996), **My Life Story**, West African Book Publishers, Limited, Ilupeju, Lagos, Nigeria, 1996.

Chapter Five

The Wide Reach of Education

Education has a wide reach with tentacles in multiple facets of human endeavor. From my perspective, the Systems view of education reaches everywhere. As has already been said, education is the star of this book. Embracing the systems view of education, it can be seen that education benefits us in diverse ways. The testimonies, stories, and narrations in this chapter bear out the multi-faceted paths to the benefits of education, not only at Saint Finbarr's College, but also at other educational institutions. Recalling my own experience, I have been advocating for education for over fifty years. That is ever since I was seventeen years old.

To make the limited education budget dollars to go further, more bangs for the buck, so to speak, we must pursue more innovations in education. Innovation can focus on a process of accomplishing an objective rather than developing a technological gadgetry (Badiru, 2020). In a 2019 journal article in the *International Journal of Quality Engineering and Technology*, I presented what I call the umbrella theory of innovation (Badiru, 2019a), in which process innovation is as important as technology innovation. Innovation in the education process can be as simple as putting the right instructor, adequately prepared, resourced, and empowered, in front of the classroom. Veteran teachers, because of their disciplined approach, broad-based education, training, service experience, wide range of practical knowledge, and story-telling ability, are most suited for delivering effective education, taking advantage of how we learn and retain information in the modern fast-paced, volatile, and dynamic social settings. I was a beneficiary of such an enhanced classroom environment, having been taught by superb teachers, who inspired me in my early engineering courses at Tennessee Technological University. I entered the teaching profession myself on the basis of my positive classroom experiences throughout my elementary, high school, and university education. My goal now is to spread the word about the diverse values of education in any society. An educated population is an essential foundation for building a stronger national defense. With education and the analytical thinking therein contained, a force of one could overcome a force of a thousand enemies. Manufacturing and enterprises within any national economic development plan depend on a solid foundation of education of the workforce (Badiru, Ibidapo-Obe, and Ayeni (2019).

The blessings of Saint Finbarr's College continued to follow me into the years beyond high school. While I was still working at Lagos State Ministry of Education, I came across an advertisement for clerks at Central Bank of Nigeria (CBN). I applied and was fortunate to secure employment as Clerk Grade C. I was posted to the Staff Pay Office. I joined CBN in April 1974. Iswat was still working at the ministry. But CBN was a short trekking distance from the ministry. So, we did not feel physically disconnected. It was at Central Ban that I met Mr. Supo Adedeji (now late), who later became a close friend and a selfless helper in my pursuits of overseas scholarships later on. I was not thinking of an immediate departure for overseas studies because I was thinking of settling down to raise a family, which my mother excitedly wanted.

Central Bank was conducting a certificate review of all staff sometime late in 1974. That was when several senior administrators came in contact with my school cert results. I was summoned to the office of Alhaji Elias, who was then a department head. He chastised me for not putting my high school performance to good use. He felt such a school cert result should be leveraged to pursue further studies overseas. I told him I was planning to go abroad for further studies, but I had not saved enough money yet. My family members were already concerned that I was whiling away my post-secondary schools. It was suspected that I was getting carried away with the fun life of Lagos and was not interested in furthering my education. Alhaji Elias' concern only served to confirm the fears of my family. He insisted that I must apply for scholarships to facilitate my further studies forthwith. When I subsequently secured Federal Government scholarships, he willingly served as one of my guarantors. Other individuals serving as my guarantors for the scholarship offers were Mr. Nupo Samuel and my brother, the Late Mr. Atanda Badiru. Father Slattery continued to provide written testimonials as required for many of my scholarship and university admission processes. Such was his dedication to the welfare and success of his students that he always found the time to provide written recommendations.

In December 1975, I proceeded to the USA to start my studies in Industrial Engineering at Tennessee Technological University. I was on a full scholarship from the Federal Government of Nigeria. Iswat came to join me in the USA in June 1976. So began my academic and professional pursuits in the USA. The sojourn started with a grand sendoff party by my Central Bank buddies. In the USA, I reconnected with the late Mr. Francis Osili, a close friend in my Central Bank office. He went to study in Wisconsin while I went to study in Tennessee. We had many years of social exchanges until his passing in 2017. May his generous soul rest in peace.

In Summer 1984, I visited Nigeria for the first time in eight years.; my first visit home after going to the USA in December1975. It was during that visit that my sister reunited me with Father Slattery. She was very proud of my academic achievement in the USA and wanted Father Slattery to be aware of what I had accomplished so far. We visited Father Slattery at his Akoka home. He had been displaced as the principal of the Saint Finbarr's College by that time. It was a very sad feeling for me to see him not on the school compound, but in a secluded house. No longer was he engaged in doing what he loved most – running Saint Finbarr's College. He recounted how bored he was for not being involved in school affairs. But at the same time, he was grateful that he then had time to devote more energy to the Church.

During the visit, Father Slattery instructed me to consolidate whatever I was planning to do on behalf of SFCOBA with what Segun was already doing. He was full of praise for Segun and his exceptional leadership skills. Since that time, Segun and I have worked closely with other dedicated Finbarrians to advance the cause of SFCOBA and the school.

I entered the academic career primarily because of my interest in following the educational lineage established by Reverend Father Slattery.

Later on, as Dean of University College at the University of Oklahoma, I tried my best to help students, foreigners and Americans alike, with their educational objectives. This created an immense gratification for me. One enters the teaching profession, not because of the financial rewards possible, but because of the opportunity to impart knowledge to others. "Teach onto others as you have been taught" is my premise for teaching. I have continued this same philosophy in all my professional pursuits.

On October 1, 1998, several Old Boys and I were inducted into the esteemed order of "Distinguished Conqueror (DC)" of Saint Finbarr's College, an exalted position of recognition for Finbarr's Alumni. Friends and family members accompanied me to the event at Sheraton Hotel. The installation accompanied the establishment of the annual distinguished lecture series, which took place on October 7, 1998. Prof. Awele Maduemezia was the main inaugural speaker. Father Slattery's public-domain speech delivered at the inaugural lecture typified his life-long service to Nigeria. He was in Ireland at the time and could not attend to deliver the speech in person. He sent the written speech (uncopyrighted and unrestricted) to officers of SFCOBA (including me) to deliver it on his behalf (in absentia). The power of the words contained in the prepared speech represented him so very well, as if he was there in person. My recollection of what I and others delivered on his behalf, under the leadership of Mr. Segun Ajanlekoko, is echoed here.

> "Welcome to all – distinguished lecturer, parents, audience and students. Many months ago, the President of St. Finbarr's, Segun Ajanlekoko, told me that the Executive Committee of the Finbarr's Old Boys were planning on inaugurating an annual distinguished guest lecture. To be truthful, I pooh-poohed the whole idea. I asked myself how a comparatively young College could launch such an august event in a city like Lagos, where there are many educational colleges and universities of great distinction. Is St. Finbarr's going to be the first college to honor their first Principal? Why? The more I thought about it, the more I realized that the proposed lecturer of today has launched, I am sure,

many First Lectures before now. But it occurs to me that it is the first time that a secondary school Principal was to be honored by past pupils in this way.

Today's Guest Speaker is Professor Awele Maduemezia, the former Vice-Chancellor of Edo State University, Ekpoma. Our speaker today is the first Nigerian to gain a Ph.D. in Physics. Another Professor – an Old Boy – will be honored with A.D.C. (Distinguished Conqueror Award). This will be the first time that your first Principal does not know personally the distinguished lecturer. You are welcome, Sir. The topic is "Education, Yesterday Years, Today, and Tomorrow." I do not want to pre-empt one iota what the lecturer will say in his lecture, but I will still say that the vast majority of those educated "Yesterday Years" were educated on a par with the present school system.

Long before I came to Nigeria in 1941, there was a Reverend Father Stephen Woodley, SMA, born in 1887 at Chester in the Diocese of Shrewsbury, England. He came at a time when nearly all the priests were continentals. The colonial Government launched great pressure on the missionaries to supply English-speaking priests and Reverend Sisters, capable of running good schools. Father Stephen Woodley was there-and-then appointed in charge of the Catholic schools in Lagos and environs. The imbalance in the number of Catholic schools and the Government schools soon became very apparent. There were 34 schools with nearly 4000 pupils only. Eleven of these schools were under the colonial Government.

The Head Masters and the teachers were certified native teachers, but in the Girls' schools, each student was taught by a European Sister.

In the Grammar School (at Holy Cross), Reverend Father Herber, SMA, taught Latin and French languages and the Principal, Father Woodley himself, took higher classes in the different English branches. Herewith, a sentence recorded in the Archives: 'The Catholic Schools in Lagos can compare favorably with the best schools in the country and our boys are admired by all … for their spirit of obedience and discipline. The above were the children of Yesterday. What of the children of Today? They were more fortunate. Our children of Today received a more thorough education parallel with the English school system. The archives tell us that Father Woodley held that post up to 1927 and enjoyed good health. He set a glorious example by building new schools and colleges, taking an interest also in games, especially in soccer. Unfortunately, in that year 1927, he was injured in the back and had to return to England. At that time, both the policy of the Church and the colonials realized that education must be urgently pursued. Many young Catholic priests gave their lives, stricken down by Yellow Fever, Black Water Fever, and Malaria, having lived only for a few years in tropical Nigeria.

Yet, it could be said that the pupils of Today (1930-1960), both at the primary school level, the secondary school and teacher training levels rivaled the colonial efforts to give a decent education to the rising generation at that time. Our products of Today became the basic rock of future education as we sailed into the education of "Tomorrow." At this stage – the year of Independence 1960 – Nigerians took charge of their own country and initiated a new and most daring education policy. The third education Tomorrow had arrived. There is no need to deny the fact that here in Nigeria, we followed step-by-step, the British Education Policy, punctuated with ultra-modern ideas borrowed from America and Europe. No longer did the new Ministry of Education confine our children to nine subjects. Even at the primary level, there were splits and choices up to twenty subjects. Every big subject was shrunk and all were added to the School Certificate Examination for the secondary schools; for boys and girls.

All of us now know that there are very obvious weaknesses in Tomorrow's education system, but let us leave that to our distinguished Physics lecturer. Please enlighten us all on Education Yesterday Years, Today, and Tomorrow. We anticipate you will write your own name in the pages of history by an honest analysis of nearly 140 years of education. Undoubtedly, you will lift the veil that has clouded our thinking in the past and brighten the future of the present student body. We hope that their future will be brighter and also the future of the parents who are dedicated to give the best to their children.

We pray that those in administration will be honest and not afraid to purge the canker worms that have eaten into our present efforts. After all, education is the light of the world. May it shine on all of us."

I wrote my first Finbarr's book in 2005. The book was launched with much fanfare in Lagos. Many dignitaries attended the event, including my good friend, Professor Oye Ibidapo-Obe, who served as the Chief Launcher. All proceeds from the book were donated to Saint Finbarr's College. Hundreds of copies left over after the launching were also donated to the school for a continuation of its fundraising programs. The Sunday Sun Newspaper of July 10, 2005 summarized the book-launch event with the following caption and narrative. Leaders and those in authority across the country have been urged to take something away from the lives of the founder of Saint Finbarr's College, Akoka, Yaba, Lagos, late Father Slattery and Professor Adedeji Bodunde Badiru, a professor of Industrial and Information Engineering at the University of Tennessee, Knoxville, Tennessee, USA. This charge came from the Vice Chancellor of the University of Lagos, Akoka, Professor Oye Ibidapo-Obe, while speaking at the launching of **"Blessings of a Father: A Tribute to the Life and Work of Reverend Father Slattery,"** a book authored by Professor Badiru at the Agip Recital Hall of Muson Center, Lagos.

The activities of the Saint Finbarr's College Old Boys Association North America (SFCOBA – North America) moved forward rapidly in 2001, mainly due to the reconnection efforts of Dr. John Nwofia. While I was seeking out old Boys from across the USA and Canada, Dr. John Nwofia was doing exactly this same thing out of his professional base in Nashville, Tennessee. It was in this concurrently effort that he contacted me via email in 2001 and inquired if I was interested in linking up with former students of Saint Finbarr's College. I excited responded affirmatively. We subsequently arranged reciprocal meetings at my home in Knoxville, Tennessee and his home in Nashville, Tennessee. Mr. Kenny Kuku and Mr. Olawale Adewoyin also attended those meetings and we scheduled additional meetings at Kenny's home in Atlanta and Olawale's home also in Atlanta. Frequent discussions and reconnections with additional ex-Finbarrians led to the emergence of our annual SFCOBA – America annual reunions. Annual reunions have since taken place as listed below:

Reunion 2012: Atlanta, Georgia, USA
Reunion 2013 (West Palm Beach, Florida)
Reunion 2014 (Nashville, Tennessee)
Reunion 2015 (Baltimore, Maryland)
Reunion 2016 (Houston, Texas)
Reunion 2017 (Chicago, Illinois)
Reunion 2018 (Atlanta, Georgia)
Reunion 2019 (Dayton, Ohio), hosted by yours, truly

At the 2013 Reunion, I was presented with the DJ Slattery Excellence Award by the SFCOBA North America. For this recognition, I was (and still remain) very grateful.

It was all fun, games, and reminiscing chatter at the Inaugural Annual Reunion of SFCOBA-North America in Atlanta, GA on September 1, 2012. A formal meeting was held to kick off the reunion. There was a specially-crafted celebratory cake for the occasion. After nine months of preparation, the reunion went on without a hitch. **Otunba Anthony Awofeso** and **Professor Adedeji Bodunde Badiru** headed the chronology of the Boys in attendance with their Class of 1972 lapel pins. Great thanks and appreciation go to Kenny Kuku and the Atlanta hosting committee, who worked tirelessly to ensure a smooth and successful event. Kenny ensured that we were all identifiable throughout the city of Atlanta that weekend with our Finbarr's logo'd shirts and caps. A few Finbarr's rascals showed up from all over North America to relive their glory days of Finbarr's "rascalism." Notable among this group was the famous "Like-a-Bull" (aka Likeabull), whose real-name identity can be found in Finbarr's historical records of boys who were thorns in the flesh of Finbarr's administrators.

A quick search among the insiders of the old Finbarr's era revealed the real identity of Patrick Efiom, who is now Colonel Patrick Efiom, serving in the US Army Reserve. His case proved that rascalism reformed is professionalism achieved. Likabu kept everything lively and entertaining throughout the reunion. He told hilarious stories that kept everyone in stitches of laughter. He also led the group in singing several of the old Finbarr's football fight songs. The songs came in handy during the novelty soccer match against the Atlanta Green Eagles. Several spouses were also in attendance to share in the celebration of the glory days of Finbarr's College. Later in the evening on Saturday, Sept. 1, the dance floor of the hotel got polished with shoe polish with repeated sliding of dancers' shoes. Many previously under-utilized leg muscles got stretched again by body gyrations in response to rhythmic calls of the loud speaker of the DJ. Knees long used for leisurely walking got tested on the dance floor. The knees held up well under the watchful eyes of the several physicians among the Boys in attendance. Dr. David Toks Gbadebo was particularly concerned about the quickening pace of the dancers' hearts. Fortunately, there was no cardiac emergency throughout the dance sessions. The photos that follow tell only a small part of the full story. The boys danced the night away, not missing any musical beats, as if they were trying to make up for the lost opportunity of the Finbarr's days of "bone-to-bone" dancing in the all-boys school.

The highlight of the three-day reunion was the novelty soccer match between the SFC Old Boys and the Atlanta Green Eagles, a well-regarded soccer club in Atlanta metro. On the SFC side were three of the best players that ever played for Saint Finbarr's in her glory days of soccer prowess in Nigeria. Their rusted skills got revived, if only in two-to-three-minute spurts. Dribbling and tackling skills that had been shelved for decades were brought back down to the playing level to be revalidated. It was like opening a can of worms. We had never seen so many Finbarrians pleading for substitutes (for themselves) from the sideline. Stephen Keshi, a former Finbarr's player, who went on to coach the Nigerian Green Eagles national team, telephoned during the match and wasn't pleased with how the Boys were doing. His words of encouragement and hints of brilliance were not enough to rescue the day. The Boys could muster only one goal against their opponents, who scored three goals in quick succession. Of course, the coach of the SFC side, Kenny Kuku, blamed the loss on a biased referee. He must have been recollecting a quote (attributed to the Duke of Edinburgh) found in Father Slattery's autobiography, which says, "Football is as good as its referee. A bad referee can spoil soccer." Professor Badiru also participated in the novelty soccer match, where he introduced a new principle of the

Physics of Soccer - - - "avoid the ball." In the end, the victors and vanquished got together to celebrate the friendly match. It is a wonderful football world, after all. Backed by their wives, as usual, the happy boys lined up (or, squatted) for a memorable group photo. The wives of Finbarr's Boys have always been staunchly supportive of the Finbarr's activities of the Boys. The annual Reunion gatherings and the 2016 group travel to Fermoy, Ireland for Father Slattery's posthumous birthday celebration are cogent examples of the togetherness of the Boys and the Wives. A lot of literary history exists about the past activities of SFCOBA. Under the leadership and coordination of Mr. Segun Ajanlekoko, the Finbarrian Newsletter was published for several years by the national body of SFCOBA in Lagos. Printed archival copies still exist in the possession of many SFCOBA members. Of particular interest is the 1996 issue, which celebrated Finbarr's fortieth anniversary (1956 – 1996).

Reverend Father Slattery's journey home was literally back to his home country of Ireland and response to the call of the Lord.

This chapter gives an account of how SFCOBA tried unsuccessfully to bring Father Slattery back to Nigeria. He had wanted to return to Nigeria to die. All efforts to convince the Catholic Mission to send him back to Nigeria in his final days failed.

Segun Ajanlekoko, Yinka Bashorun, and I visited Father at his Maryland (Lagos mainland) residence on his brief return to Nigeria around 1998. When he was sent back to Ireland by the Church, he very much wanted us to visit him in his retirement home in Cork, Ireland. That visit never materialized due to logistical constraints. But we continued to communicate with him by phone and mail. That gladdened his heart until his death.

This following narrative provides a documentation of Mr. Segun Ajanleko's last meeting with Father Slattery. It shows, in retrospect, what could have been a befitting grand finale of the exit of the man called Father Slattery from mother Earth in Nigeria, but it was not to be.

While in office as President of SFCOBA, Segun made it a point of duty on a weekly basis to visit Father Slattery at his St. Denis Catholic Church Home, to exchange words as well sought his guidance on matters that concerned the school, (our Alma Mater) SFCOBA, Nigeria as a nation, life in general, and, indeed, Segun's own private enterprises.

It was on one such occasion that Segun posed the question where he would like to be buried, if in accordance with his wish he died in Nigeria. He told Segun that he would like to be buried in St. Finbarr's school compound. Segun quickly responded by asking him where in particular. He replied by saying that it should be inside the retirement home that was being built for him by the SFCOBA inside the school compound.

Segun further asked him which particular spot. He then got up and asked Segun to drive him to the school compound. There and then he pointed to a spot near to his prayer room. Segun conveyed this message to the generality of the Old Boys. Thereafter, it became a project, which all Finbarrians both old and young directed all their energies to ensure would happen and be successful.

Unfortunately, after his 80th birthday in February 29, 1996, Father Slattery was asked to retire and was sent back to Cork in Ireland, where he began his ministry. But hope was not lost as it was on record that Father Slattery actually wrote his wish in his will. Segun, therefore, took it upon himself to regularly keep in touch with him on a weekly basis through telephone calls and whenever he traveled abroad, especially to Britain, he ensured that he had daily conversation with him from London.

On one occasion Segun decided to visit him in Ireland to be accompanied by the wife of one of our first-six member, Mrs. Beatrice Ozogolu, who Father Slattery had introduced to Segun as a lifesaver and whom Father Slattery told indicated had never, for once, failed to pay him a visit every month in Cork in Ireland. Her late husband was the First President of the SFCOBA. Please note that a full chapter at the end of this book is devoted to Mrs. Ozogolu's personal tribute to Father Slattery. The Ozogolu family and Father Slattery went back a long and rewarding time, as readers would find in that special chapter.

Unfortunately, the visit by Segun and Mrs. Ozogolu was not to be because Father Slattery fell ill and was hospitalized. Whenever Segun phoned him in Ireland, the discussion usually centered around Saint Finbarr's College, Saint Finbarr's Old Boys, plus of course, Segun's own family and his business. He was interested to know how the Old Boys were doing and whether they were contributing to the sustainability of the Association.

Segun recalled a famous statement by Father Slattery during one of such conversations. Father Slattery said, "whoever contributes to the growth of his old association will never go in want; he shall be blessed in multiples for he has been faithful to the cause."

And then the end came in July 2003. Segun was in Europe and tried to phone Father Slattery as was customary, but he was informed by the Seminary that he was in the hospital in an Intensive Care Unit and he could not speak to Segun. Segun got back to Lagos on July 11, 2003 to receive a message from a Rev Father, an Ex-Finbarrian, who broke the news of the passing of Father Slattery, the great man and the paternal Father that we, his students, never had.

Two things I think are worth putting down for the sake of posterity, which emanated from Segun's discussion with Father Slattery while, so to speak, he was in exile in Ireland. The same topics were discussed with me by Father Slattery whenever I exchanged communication with him in the mid to late 1990s.

(i) The first one has to do with Father Slattery's abhorrence for what he considered a confinement and solitude in the Old Monastery in Cork. He was of the view that he did not belong there as most of the people who were there had gone senile and could not engage in meaningful discussions with him. Father Slattery, up to the end, had a very sharp brain and was very vibrant at his old age. And so he felt that birds of different feathers were flocking together in the monastery!!! He wanted to get out!!!

(ii) The second has to do with his fervent and uncompromised desire to come back to Nigeria to "live" out the rest of his life in Nigeria. SFCOBA developed various strategies toward the realization of this dream. One of the strategies was to ask the Old Boys to write a letter requesting that Father Slattery should be released to us and assuring them in Ireland that he would be well taken care of by the Old Boys.

But it was not to be!!! The mission never caved in to the various repeated pleadings by the Old Boys. Meanwhile, the letter was never written, due to logistical obstacles, before the death of Father Slattery. It is a collective guilt of all the Old Boys that we had the opportunity, but we allowed the events out of our control to prevent delivering on the opportunity. Had we known that the end was near, we could have mounted a different mode of approach to get the letter written and delivered in person. So, our dear Reverend Father passed on, unsung (at that time), by those who benefited tremendously from his benevolence, his tutelage, his priesthood and his fatherly advice. If the letter had been written, it would have been another documentary evidence of the efforts made to bring Father Slattery back to Nigeria. This book and other similar efforts are designed to accomplish posthumous singing of the praises of Father Slattery.

Father Slattery has fulfilled his mission and would, no doubt, be working in the higher realms (the vineyard of the Father), where only those who have passed are granted the opportunity to belong. We, collectively, salute his great spirit!!! Live on, our dear Reverend Father Denis Joseph Slattery.

Watching us from above, we do hope that Father Slattery enjoyed the first-year anniversary celebration that was convened in his honor in 2004, under the leadership of Segun Ajanlekoko. The celebration was done in a grand style with ceremonial slaughtering of a cow. Due to the special efforts and dedication of Mr. Bosede Odelusi and his UK SFCOBA, a posthumous celebration of Father Slattery's 100th Birthday took place in his home town of Fermoy, Ireland on 27-29 February 2016. The event was attended by former students of Saint Finbarr's College from various corners of the world. My wife and I were in attendance. Several wives also accompanied their husbands to the celebration. Father Slattery's nephew, Mr. Joe Slattery and his wife, Catherine, generously hosted the Finbarr's group to a variety of Irish hospitality events. The photo journals in this chapter convey the breadth and depth of celebratory festivities. Born on 29th February 1916 (a leap year), Father Slattery would have been 100 years old on 29th February 2016, although Father Slattery, himself, would have joked to be only 25 years old, going by the celebration of his actual birth date every four years.

There is a lot that is involved in delivering and acquiring education. It is a potpourri of systems and subsystems. All of these must be in good consonance in order to achieve the intended results and success. The approach of this chapter is to look at a few specific factors that revolve around the success of a college student. Of particular interest is the interplay between innate intelligence, common sense, and self-discipline.

The moral of the introductory proclamation quotes at the beginning of this chapter is that students must be ready, adaptive, and perceptive in the educational process. They must embrace situational awareness to take advantage of the opportunities that present themselves. This is what paves the way for sustainable academic success. Surviving the rigors of education takes a good mixture of intelligence, common sense, self-discipline, and good personal organization. While much has been said and written about academic requirements, very little guidelines are available for being a personal factor in the education process itself. To be a complete educated person requires efforts outside of the conventional educational process. It should be recalled that many of the learned professionals, engineers, doctors, artists, and theologians of centuries ago were self-taught. Abraham Lincoln, a noted lawyer, was entirely self-taught. His achievements, leading to being elected the 16th president of the United States, confirmed a high level of self-discipline and common sense in addition to his native intelligence.

While attempting to make the most out of student-teacher interactions, I have found that many students lack the basic elements that facilitate the education process. Unfortunately, there are very few formal avenues for teaching students how to properly manage their academic programs. College education requires students with professional maturity, who are motivated and committed to learning. They must play an active role in their education and understand the value of learning as a life-long professional goal. They must also have a clear perception of their career and educational objectives. Each student must approach the academic challenge with dedication and utmost commitment. As an educator, I am particularly a stickler for eliciting personal responsibility from students. Students are expected to demonstrate a whole-person capability covering a variety of skills and personal attributes. Some of these include the following:

- Time consciousness
- Interpersonal etiquette
- Taking personal responsibility
- Effective communication
- Adequate preparation for class
- Good study habits
- Compliance with institutional requirements
- Conformance with social norms and standards
- Contingency planning with respect to "Murphy's Law"
- Learning to allow sufficient lead time between consecutive activities
- Planning, scheduling, and controlling study-related activities
- Managing independent assignments
- Familiarization with university resources, such as libraries, labs, etc.
- Positive interactions with other students

Most students entering college are assumed to already have a good level of academic preparation. Where they need help is with being organized and managing themselves well. Essential characteristics for success with college education include the following:

- Intelligence
- Ingenuity
- Creativity
- Self-organization and management
  - ➢ Organize, organize, organize, and organize again
- Knowing where everything is kept to minimize non-value-adding search times

Knowledge and smartness alone are not enough to succeed with college education. College students must have the skills necessary to apply knowledge and the attitude required to become responsible and ethical professionals. Skills such as those required for effective learning, problem solving, and communication cannot be learned in the traditional lecture format. Students must exhibit the motivation, self-discipline, and dedication for doing more outside class to enhance classroom success.

Maslow's Hierarchy of Needs

Education is the most stable investment in securing a satisfying future. A needs-based assessment of personal drive is essential to pursuing college education. Self-motivation and commitment will enhance the ability to meet personal needs. The student's personal social needs should be taken into account in the education process. **Maslow's "Hierarchy of Needs"** suggests the following categories as possible drivers for adapting to the hierarchical demands of college education:

Physiological Needs: The needs for the basic things of life; such as food, water, housing, and clothing. This is the level where access to money is most critical.

Safety Needs: The needs for security, stability, and freedom from threat of physical harm. The fear of adverse environmental impact may inhibit project efforts.

Social Needs: The needs for social approval, friends, love, affection, and association. For example, public service projects may bring about better economic outlook that may enable individuals to be in a better position to meet their social needs.

Esteem Needs: The needs for accomplishment, respect, recognition, attention, and appreciation. These needs are important not only at the individual level, but also at the national level.

Self-actualization Needs: These are the needs for self-fulfillment and self-improvement. They also involve the availability of opportunity to grow professionally. Improvement projects on the job may lead to self-actualization opportunities for individuals to assert themselves socially and economically. Job achievement and professional recognition are two of the most important factors that lead to employee satisfaction and better motivation. Education is a sustainable platform for meeting the needs of each individual.

Hierarchical motivation implies that the particular motivation technique utilized for a given person should depend on where the person stands in the hierarchy of needs listed above. For example, the needs for esteem take precedence over the physiological needs when the latter are relatively well satisfied. Money, for example, cannot be expected to be a very successful motivational factor for an individual who is already on the fourth level of the hierarchy of needs.

Educational Motivators

Motivation can involve the characteristics of the education process itself. In the theory of motivation, there are two motivational factors classified as the hygiene factors and motivators. Hygiene factors are necessary but not sufficient conditions for a contented individual. The negative aspects of the factors may lead to a disgruntled person, whereas their positive aspects do not necessarily enhance the satisfaction of the person. Examples include:

Educational policies: Bad policies can lead to the discontent of individuals while good policies are viewed as routine with no specific contribution to improving satisfaction.

Academic supervisor: A bad supervisor can make a person unhappy and less productive while a good supervisor cannot necessarily improve person's performance.

Working condition: Bad working conditions can impede students, but good conditions do not automatically generate improved productivity.

Study environment: A bad study environment can adversely affect student performance, but a good study environment does not, by default, improve student performance. There must be an external stimulus or driver for the student's higher performance.

Income: Low income can make a person unhappy, disruptive, and uncooperative, but an increase in income will not necessarily induce him or her to perform better. While a raise in salary will not necessarily increase professionalism, a reduction in salary will most certainly have an adverse effect on morale.

Social life: A miserable social life can adversely affect academic performance, but a happy social life does not imply better academic performance.

Interpersonal relationships: Good peer, superior, and subordinate relationships are important to keep a person happy and productive, but extraordinarily good relationships do not guarantee that he or she would be more productive.

Social and professional status: A low status can make a person to devolve to performing at his or her "level" whereas a higher status does not imply that he or she will perform at a higher level.

Security: A safe environment may not motivate a person to perform better, but an unsafe condition will certainly impede productivity.

Motivators are motivating agents that should be inherent in the work or study environment. If necessary, work should be redesigned to include inherent motivating factors. Some guidelines for incorporating motivators into jobs are presented below:

Achievement: The academic study process should incorporate opportunities for achievement and avenues to set personal goals to excel.

Recognition: The mechanism for recognizing superior performance should be incorporated into the study process. Opportunities for recognition should be built into the overall academic process.

Curriculum content: The curriculum work content should be interesting enough to motivate and stimulate the creativity of the individual. The amount of work and the organization of the work should be designed to fit the student's needs.

Responsibility: An individual should have some measure of responsibility for how his or her goals are pursued. Personal responsibility leads to accountability, which yields better performance. In this respect, a student should take responsibility for his or her academic performance.

Professional growth: The curriculum work should offer an opportunity for advancement so that the individual can set his or her own achievement level for professional growth within a reasonable plan of study.

The above examples may be described as study or work enrichment approaches with the basic philosophy that work or study can be made more interesting in order to induce an individual to perform at a higher level.

An educational goal consists of a detailed description of the overall pursuit and expectations from an academic pursuit. A goal is the composite effect of a series of objectives. Each objective should be defined with respect to its implication on the career goal of the student. A goal analysis helps to determine the courses of action with respect to what courses to take, what major to choose, and what project options to explore. A goal-clarification approach should be used to set educational goals and objectives. This approach focuses on identifying specific goals and objectives that will assure success. Implementing the objectives, tracking performance over time, and providing ongoing assessment of strengths and weaknesses can help students set and enhance their goals. Business techniques such as "management by objectives" and "value stream mapping" can be used during the education planning process.

Adequate training is essential because it prepares students to do their jobs well by building the right knowledge that permits logical actions and decision making. If the right skills are provided for students, they can develop efficient work habits and positive attitudes that promote cooperation and teamwork for academic study and career paths. Some approaches to training as a complement to strict academic study are described below:

- Formal education in an academic institution
- On-the-job training through hands-on practice
- Continuing education short courses
- Training videos
- Group training seminars
- Role playing games

Some important aspects of setting educational goals and objectives include the following:

- Appraise existing categories and levels of technical skills.
- Consider the skills that would be needed in the future.
- Consider the possible career options.
- Appreciate the prevailing global workplace.
- Assess a combination of domestic and study-abroad opportunities.
- Leverage the infrastructure of existing technical training centers.
- Screen, select, and map skills, aptitude, and interests to training opportunities.
- Monitor progress and modify training process as needed.
- Synchronize the inflow and outflow of trainees with job potentials and national needs.
- Place trained manpower in relevant job functions.
- Leverage the working experience of professionals to guide education and training programs.
- Use documentations of results as inputs for planning future training programs.

The pursuit of education may be driven by the need for knowledge or the need for future income potential. In each case, the education objectives must be compatible with the characteristics and intrinsic attributes of the individual. Many changes are now occurring in academic programs in preparation for the future work place, which has become a benchmark for many strategic planners.

Are we all ready for the future work environment?

Is the present education process aligned with the future needs?

As the business world prepares to meet the technological challenges of the future, there is a need to focus on the people who will take it there. People will be the most important component of the "man-machine-material" systems that will compete in the future work place. Graduate and undergraduate educators should play a crucial role in preparing the work force for the future through their roles as change initiators and facilitators. Improvements are needed in undergraduate education to facilitate a solid graduate education.

Undergraduate education is the foundation for professional practice. Undergraduate programs are the basis for entry into graduate schools and other professional fields. To facilitate this transition, curriculum and process improvements are needed in education strategies. Educators, employers, and practitioners advocate better integration of Science, Technology, Engineering, and Mathematics (STEM) with the concepts of design and practice throughout university education. Such integration should be a key component of any education reform. Hurried attempts to improve education are being made in many areas. We now have terms like "Total Quality Management for Academia", "Just-in-Time Education," "Outcome-Based Education," and "Continuous Education Improvement." Unfortunately, many of these represent mere rhetoric that is not backed by practical implementation strategies or a funding base.

Incorporating quality concepts into education is a goal that should be pursued at national, state, local, and institutional levels. Existing business models of quality management and continuous improvement can be adopted for curriculum improvement. However, because of the unique nature of academia, a re-definition of the business approaches will be necessary, so that the techniques will be compatible with the academic process. The basic concepts of improving product quality are applicable to improving any education process. A careful review of STEM curricula will reveal potential areas for improvement. This will help avoid stale curricula that may not adequately meet current and future needs of the society. For example, the basic scope of STEM education should be expanded to incorporate and embrace liberal arts and other social science areas that are very vital for the advancement of the society as a whole. This author has seen recent efforts by some schools to expand the STEM programs to STEMMA (Science, Technology, Engineering, Medicine, and Arts). This is a more robust approach to improving the education process.

The following specific symptoms of educational challenges have been noted:

- Increasing undergraduate attrition despite falling academic standards at many schools
- Decreasing teaching loads in favor of increasing dedication to research in higher education

- Migration of full professors from undergraduate teaching in favor of graduate teaching, sponsored research, and research center administration
- Watered down contents of undergraduate courses in the attempt to achieve retention goals
- Decreasing relevance of undergraduate courses to real-world practice
- Decreasing communication skills of college graduates
- Language is the expression of our thoughts in words. Grammar is the science of languages, and the art of speaking and writing correctly. If communication skills degrade, the expression of thought could be faulty.

Professional morality and responsibility should be introduced early to college students. Lessons on ethics should be incorporated into curriculum improvement approaches. Students should have a basic understanding of ethics and should appreciate the following requirements:

- Use knowledge and skill for the enhancement of human welfare.
- Be honest, loyal, and impartial in serving the public, employers, and colleagues.
- Strive to increase the competence and prestige of the chosen profession.
- Support and participate in the activities of professional and technical societies.

Life-long Education

Education should not just be a matter of taking courses, getting good grades, and moving on. Life-long lessons should be a basic component of every education process. These lessons can only be achieved through a Systems view of education. The politics of practice should be explained to students so that they are not shocked and frustrated when they go from the classroom to the boardroom.

Universities face a variety of real-world multi-disciplinary problems that are often similar to business operations problems. These problems could be used as test cases for solution approaches. Interdisciplinary student teams should be formed to develop effective solutions to societal problems. I summarize my own view as shown below:

There is never one perfect solution;
There is never one single solution;
Only an integrated systems-focused solution can get us to our goals of solving societal problems.

Schools should increase their interactions with local businesses and industry, when available and possible. This will facilitate more realistic and relevant joint projects for students and working professionals.

The versatility of university education can be enhanced by encouraging students to take more cross-disciplinary courses to facilitate the interplay of STEM areas and liberal arts. Students must keep in mind that computer is just a tool and not the solution. For example, a word processor is a clerical tool that cannot compose a report by itself without the creative thinking and writing ability of the user. Likewise, a spreadsheet program is an analytical tool that cannot perform accurate calculations without accurate inputs from the user. Undergraduate and graduate education should be seen as contiguous components in the overall hierarchy of education process.

Measured quantitatively by IQ (Intelligence Quotient), natural intelligence is what makes a person self-aware and adaptive to the ambient stimuli. Even the highest level of intelligence does not guarantee success unless it is applied on a bed rock of common sense and self-discipline.

Achieving success with getting things done is actually simple, if one initiates success right from the beginning. All it takes are a few key ground rules and perseverance, such as those listed below:

- Exercising commitment
- Exhibiting fortitude
- Extending compromise
- Demonstrating selectivity is what is done
- Embracing delegation when appropriate
- Displaying diligence
- Showing perseverance

- Teaming and partnering through:
  o Communication
  o Cooperation
  o Coordination
- Using the right tools
- Timing of what is done
- Outsourcing what is better done elsewhere

Maximize the utilization of each available hour of each day. Do, during the day, what you need daylight or working hours to do. Conversely, do not do, during the day, what you don't need daylight or working hours to do. In other words, use daylight hours appropriately to perform tasks that truly need daylight hours and put off until after-hours, those things that can be done at off hours.

Outsource tasks for which you have no skills, tools, or time; or from which you do not derive enjoyment or gratification. But you must retain control of accountability for the tasks.

In order to do certain types of projects right, you must get the right person to do it. Don't over-indulge in DIY (Do-It-Yourself) mentality on all things. Some things are better done by those who know what they are doing; and those who have the right tools.

Even good projects can go bad for several reasons including the following:

- Ineffective management of requirements
- Inadequate risk appreciation and management
- Improper scope management
- Lack of full commitment
- Lack of streamlining
- Unrealistic expectations
- Action bluffing with no real action

When multi-tasking, we must evaluate what should have priority. An assessment of what is important versus what is urgent will help identify priority items. Not all tasks can be of equal "high" priority. What is important is not necessarily urgent; and what we often perceive as urgent is not really important. Tasks that are important and urgent have high priority. Those with low urgency and low importance fall in the "ignore" region; and do not deserve much attention in the overall scheme of things. Unfortunately, our lives are often ruled by urgency. With proper project management techniques, we can manage priorities by trading-off between what is urgent and what is important.

Many little choices that we make about what we do or don't do ultimately affect execution of projects. Make healthy personal choices; and you remain healthy to execute your projects successfully. Make personal bad choices, and they will come back to haunt you. Poor health and sour outlook impede the ability to execute projects efficiently.

Take care of yourself so that you can take care of your tasks. Likewise, take care of your means of transportation. Take care of your car so that you can get to where you need to be promptly to do what you need to do in a timely manner. Many of our projects these days depend on accessible modes of transportation. Thus, project implementation can be very car-dependent. Getting to work on time, arriving on time for appointments, reaching a destination safe all can be impacted by the operational condition of our vehicles. For example, if we get our vehicles ready for harsh winter conditions, we will experience fewer car-related project delays. Winter transportation problems can be preempted by getting our cars ready for winter by doing the following:

- Service and maintain radiator system
- Replace windshield-wiper fluid with appropriate winter mixture
- Check tire pressure regularly
- Invest in replacing worn tires
- Maintain full tank of fuel during winter months to keep ice from forming in the tank and fuel lines
- Have ice scrapers accessible within passenger space in the vehicle; not stored in the trunk

Practicing Self-Regulation

Practicing self-regulation requires a high degree of self-discipline. Have you ever considered yourself as a resource for your projects? That is, a resource that should be managed and regulated? Taking care of oneself is a direct example of human resource management, which is crucial for project success. Proper diet, exercise, and sleep are essential for mental alertness and positively impact the ability to get things done. Sleep, for example, affects many aspects of mental and physical activities. Sleep more and you will be amazed that you can get more done. This is because being well rested translates to fewer errors and preempts the need for rejects and rework. The notion that you have to stay up to get more done is not necessarily always true. Likewise, keep fit and get more done. Studies have confirmed that fit kids get better grades in school. Similarly, physically fit adults have been found to advance more professionally.

It is imperative to avoid "management by bluffing." It is not always easy to accomplish what you "bluff" to do. Thus, cutting down on "action bluffing" and being selective with pledges will help streamline the list of things to do. Like an old IBM commercial said, "Stop talking. Start doing." This statement suggests the need to move on to the implementation stage of what needs to be done. Plans formulated so beautifully on paper or articulated in words mean nothing if they cannot be implemented.

In addition to overall strategies for getting to where we want to be, there must be tactical actions for getting there. This, essentially, is the purpose of project management. Project management is about creating the building blocks, called Work Breakdown Structure (WBS), that serve as steps toward the eventual project goal. Each element of the WBS represents something that must be done. Project management helps in getting those things done. That means we get things done through project management. WBS facilitates breaking a project up into manageable chunks. Project partition or segmentation improves overall project control at the operational level.

It is a fact that success can only be assured through dealing with manageable sets of tasks and activities. Whenever possible, consolidate activities. If we attempt to tackle multi-dimensional solutions that will require many players and participants, it would be more difficult to get everything to come together.

Strategy is the vehicle for closing the gap between the current state and a desired future state. In order to build an effective strategy, we must have a honest assessment of the current state and a realistic evaluation of what can be achieved from that current state. For example, if current annual income is

$75,000.00 and it is desirable to move up to $85,000.00, a strategy must be developed to close that gap. It is obvious that the strategy to be developed will be a function of the two end-points. If the disjoint between the two end points cannot be resolved, no amount of strategizing can close the inherent gap. Once a strategy has been formulated, the techniques of project management will be needed to actually implement the strategy. Thus, Strategy Building and Project Management are intimately tied together. They jointly produce desired results.

Project management is the vehicle of strategy. You cannot have a strategy without project management. Likewise, you cannot have project management without it being tied to a strategy. In the corporate world, much is made of the process of business strategy development; without a concerted effort toward project management. No wonder many corporate strategies fail.

In between strategy and project management lie risks. Every endeavor is subject to risks. If there were no risks, there would be no actions. Risks create opportunities. We must appreciate the risks that our projects portend and develop appropriate strategies to mitigate the risks. We must learn to strategize, streamline, and integrate project activities.

Always weigh cost versus time, cost versus quality, and time versus quality. Preempt problems by using multi-dimensional decision analysis. A simple example is a trade-off decision analysis of traveling by air or by road. The objective here is to get the travel done subject to the nuances of cost, time, and quality; which form the so-called concept of the "Iron Triangle," also known as "Triple Constraints," which examines the trade-offs between cost, time, and quality or budget, schedule, and performance. The cliché in this respect is "cost, time, quality; which two do you want?" This implies that all three cannot be satisfied at equal levels. So, a trade-off or compromise must be exercised.

Haste makes waste and rush makes crash. In over 37 years of driving on local, rural, back-road, and interstate roadways all over the USA, this author has never been involved in any type of accident (knock on wood); not even fender-benders. He has defensive and avoidance driving habits to avert being involved in accidents. Simple practices such as not following too close, not over-speeding, and being courteous to other drivers can significantly increase the chances of not being involved in an accident. It "takes two to tangle," and if one partner is unwilling and uncooperative in the tangling act, road collisions can be minimized. The last time this author was pulled over for traffic offense was in 1982 on Interstate 75 somewhere in Georgia, doing 71 where 55 was the limit. He still believes the stoppage was unjustified and was instigated by the fact that he was driving his beloved "hot rod" aka 1976 Chevy Camaro Rally Sport. He was pulled over from a long stretch of vehicles moving about the same speed. In other words, he was going with the traffic flow. He vowed since then never to allow himself to be subjected to any other unjustified traffic pull-over. He has respected and honored that vow ever since as a show of **self-discipline**. He refers to his conservative driving habits as simply "respecting yourself" so that others (especially the cops) can respect your space and time.

A couple of hours spent attending to being stopped by a state trooper or sorting out accident details are hours taken away from some other projects. Over the years, this author has been asked how he manages to get so many things done so effortlessly. His usual response is "project management and problem preemption" This simply means using problem preemption techniques to avoid distractions that impede desired projects. Problem avoidance makes it possible to devote time to and focus on activities that really matter for project execution purposes.

Playing by the rule up front saves time later on to get things done. Circumventing rules to cut corners can only lead to distractions and the need for time-consuming amendment later on. Time and effort invested in complying with rules and conforming to requirements pays off in the long run. I describe myself as being a "self-imposed compliant conformist." This is a strategy that works by preempting trouble spots that would otherwise require resolution time. There will sometimes be a need for more time-consuming prudence in dotting all i's and crossing all t's upfront before concluding a deal, whatever the "deal" might be. If the prudence is not exercised upfront, it may come back to cause time-consuming resolution attempts and delays later on.

In the final analysis of getting things done intelligently, the basic approach is to get on with it. There is never a perfect time to get something done. Each opportunity comes with its own constraints. Each constraint may entail its own certain level of necessity. This may be a necessity that must be attended to; such that avoiding the constraints is not possible. If one waits for the perfect time, most things will never get done. We must be willing to compromise, accept trade-offs, and move on.

"The three great essentials to achieve anything worthwhile are, first, hard work; second, stick-to-itiveness; third, common sense." - Thomas A. Edison

"Common sense is in spite of, not the result of, education." - Victor Hugo

Common sense requires all five senses. To develop and apply common sense, a student must "feel" his or her environment as enumerated below:

> Look to see what is around you.
> Listen to hear the sounds of the environment.
> Touch to appreciate the texture of the surroundings.
> Smell the scents of the environment. "Smell the roses," so to speak.
> Taste to appreciate what is available to you.

Obviously, for each individual, the strength of one sense may be higher than the others. Nature has a way of making amendments, such that internal compensations take place to the extent that the overall capability of the individual may still be enhanced. Balancing is essential in education.

A student must balance personal engagements through study, work, and play. You must keep your feet properly planted on the tasks that matter and avoid falling over the edge of the steps of project management. In project management, one must deal with multiple objectives that often compete for time and resources. This is particularly critical when balancing regular work objectives with irregular personal objectives.

By using project management techniques, one set of objectives can be coordinated to support another set of objectives, and vice versa. A key requirement is to determine where and when compromises are possible and to what extent to exercise the compromises; particularly where work life versus home life is an issue.

Take time to get things done right the first time. Haste makes waste and leads to non-value-adding corrective actions later on. You are your own best advocate. Humans have morbid fascination with other's failure, tragedy, and accidents. Don't allow your project to create a spectacle for rubber-necking onlookers.

Mistakes are essential for learning and learning is essential for future project success. Plan what you need to do. Execute as planned. Learn from the project and document lessons learned. It is essential to close out a task. Closing a project is as important as initiating it. Not closing a task promptly often leads to project failure. Use the close-out to plan and initiate the next project. This process is summarized in the PELC (Plan-Execute-Learn-Close) quadrants of project success. While preparing for mistakes, we must also take precautions. As it is often said, **"measure twice and cut once."** Precautions that are taken to preempt errors result in saving time. Time, thus saved, can be redirected at more productive activities. Resources are scarce and we should not engage in wasteful mistakes.

Don't let unproductive activities "occupy" your time. These are activities that spread their "tentacles" throughout the span of a student's responsibilities. They become operational cancers that are difficult to eradicate. They can creep into every facet of your life without providing justification for their continuation and without any value-adding basis. If these time robbers are not avoided or terminated, they continue to consume time and resources while detracting from valuable accomplishments.

Getting more things done requires focusing on fewer things to do. Never spend time and effort on an activity that has little or no potential for providing value or generating a benefit. This implies that we must "separate the wheat from the chaff," when deciding on what needs to be done. We must be able to distinguish value-adding activities from wasteful activities. That means, we must operate "lean" and cut out non-value-adding activities. As much as 80% of our activities could be going into wasteful engagements.

Attempting to do too much often leads to less being done. Tackling too much makes the "doer" more error prone, thereby leading to rework and subsequent waste of corrective time. The Pareto distribution is often extended to what is called ABC analysis, whereby items are organized into A, B, and C categories. These can be explained as follows:

A Category: Top 10% in order of value (absolutely essential).

B Category: Middle 80% in order of value (essential).

C Category: Bottom 10% in order of value (non-essential).

The C Category is often a "lost cause" and can be eliminated without much adverse consequence. By eliminating this, you will have more time to focus on the essential items. You will, consequently, be getting more done by focusing on fewer essential items.

Too often in life, we allow inconsequential lifestyles activities to rob us of time to get *really* valuable things done. You cannot hem-and-haw all day and then complain that you don't have enough time to get things done. Dilly-dally and shilly-shally ways of life rob us of opportunities to get the right things done promptly and satisfactorily. Below is my first principle of getting things done.

"To get more done, try and do less."

There are little nagging things that consume time every day. They are usually of little or no value. Eliminate them and you will have more discretionary time to yourself. Saving time through project management gives you time to do other things that you really want to do. If Albert Einstein had attempted to do several things in the years that he was fiddling with his theory of relativity, he probably would not have gotten it done when he did. Leonardo da Vinci (of the Mona Lisa fame) was reputed to not have been a good project manager because he died with several unfinished projects in various stages of incompleteness. What would have happened if he had focused on a few projects that were actually finished?

In order to get more done, you need to be more selective with social impositions. Such impositions create more things to do and less time to do the most crucial tasks. You don't have to visit Joe and Jane every time they issue an invitation for a gathering. You don't really have to attend every social function for which you have an invitation, no matter how sumptuous the Hors D'oeuvres might be. Identify what not to do at all. Identify what to do and in what order. Set goals and hold firm to the goals. Flip-flopping between setting goals and dismantling them with inaction does not leave room for actually getting things done.

Get started promptly with whatever needs to be done. What is worth doing is worth doing at the earliest opportunity. The old adage of "early to bed, early to rise" is very applicable to managing projects effectively and getting things done. The best things in life are done early in the morning. Milking cow is a good example. By contrast, most evils occur at night. The occurrence of crime is a good example. Farmers happily embrace the "early start" adage; and that is why this author loves farmers. The USA Army used to advertise that they "get more done before 9a.m. than most people get done all day." That is, indeed, the truth; and that is why this author loves the military. But the Army advertisement was phased out when it was realized that the young people of nowadays, who were being targeted as recruits, were not in favor of doing much early in the morning; if at all they get up that early. It is sad that the old adage of starting early has been replaced by the new truism of putting things off as late as possible. It is hoped that the lessons provided in this book will encourage readers to recapture the essence of what got our forefathers to the exalted level of work ethics that they handed down to us.

Discipline is a key topic of this book. Discipline is within your control. But it requires dedication, commitment, positive attitude, seriousness, and perseverance.

Success comes from self-discipline.

Self-discipline is a cornerstone of sustainable success.

Discipline is what helps you to get up in the morning to go to class when you'd rather continue to sleep.

Discipline is what helps you to overcome uninvited temptation.

Yes, refusing temptation is within your control.

Discipline helps you avoid over-drinking, over-eating, over-spending, and other undesirable indulgences.

Be mindful that "five minutes of temporary pleasure can lead to everlasting sorrow." Don't put the fun before the pain.

The single most important requirement for getting things done is self-commitment. It is through the discipline of self-commitment that projects, both large and small, can be executed successfully. Without self-commitment to do what needs to be done when it needs to be done, nothing can be accomplished satisfactorily. As a case in point, the number of those getting project management training and certification is increasing rapidly. Yet, the number of project failures, with significant cost, schedule, and performance implications, is also increasing. This is a fact that is inconsistent with theory and conventional expectation. If there is no self-commitment to execute a project according to plan, no amount of education, training, credentialing, tools, and techniques can rescue the project. Those who are most eloquent about what needs to be done, and how, are often the ones who falter when it comes to actually doing it. Each person must self-dedicate and self-actuate to make commitment to get things done the way they ought to be done.

Japanese 5s Methodology

Nothing demonstrates self-discipline more than being organized. There are all kinds of guides for getting organized. In the corporate environment, there are formal tools and techniques of pursuing a disciplined approach to work. In this section, I leverage the rigorous Japanese technique of 5s. The belief is that these tools, applied on the small scale of personal needs, would be just as effective as they have been in the corporate work environment.

The "5s" methodology (Badiru, 2019b) is Japanese technique that demonstrates work place discipline through a series of words starting with the letter "s."

1. **Seiri (Sort):** This means distinguish between what is needed and not needed and remove the latter. The tools and materials in the workplace are sorted out. The unwanted tools and materials are placed in the tag area.

2. **Seiton (Stabilize):** This means to enforce a place for everything and everything in its place. The workplace is organized by labeling. The

machines and tools are labeled with their names and all the sufficient data required. A sketch with exact scale of the work floor is drawn with grids. This helps in achieving a better flow of work and easy access of all tools and machines.

3. **Seison (Shine):** This means to clean up the workplace and look for ways to keep it clean. Periodic cleaning and maintenance of the workplace and machines are done. The wastes are placed in a separate area. The recyclable and other wastes are separately placed in separate containers. This makes it easy to know where every component is placed. The clean look of the work place helps in a better organization and increases flow.

4. **Seiketsu (Standardize):** This means to maintain and monitor adherence to the first three s's. This process helps to standardize work. The work of each person is clearly defined. The suitable person is chosen for a particular work. People in the workplace should know who is responsible for what. The scheduling is standardized. Time is maintained for every work that is to be done. A set of rules is created to maintain the first 3s's. This helps in improving efficiency of the workplace.

5. **Shitsuke (Sustain):** This means to follow the rules to keep the workplace 5s-compliant — "maintain the gain." Once the previous 4s's are implemented some rules are developed for sustaining the other S's.

In many organizational applications of 5s, it is sometimes necessary or expedient to extend the methodology to include additional areas of "s," as listed below:

> **Safety:** This refers to eliminating hazards in the work environment. The sixth "s" is added so that focus could be directed at safety within all improvement efforts. This is particularly essential in high-risk and accident-prone environments. This sixth extension is often debated as a separate entity because safety should be implicit in everything we do. Besides, the Japanese word for Safety is "Anzen," which does not follow the "s" rhythm. Going further out on a limp, some practitioners even include additional "s's".

So, we could have 8s with the addition of Security and Satisfaction.

Security (e.g., job security, personal security, mitigation of risk, capital security, intellectual security, property security, information security, asset security, equity security, product brand security, etc.)

Satisfaction (e.g., employee satisfaction, morale, job satisfaction, sense of belonging, etc.)

Thus, we sometimes see "6s" or "8s" methodologies.

How to apply self-discipline

- Think of the possible consequence of your actions.
- Don't let friends, leisure, and recreation "occupy" too much of your study time.

Badiru's Four Read-Through Guide: This is my discipline-based guide for taking a test. It centers on reading a test question thoroughly before attempting to solve the test problem. Read a test question again and again before attempting to answer the question. The four-read-through guide suggests reading a test question four times and it goes as follows:

- Read the test question for the first time, just for general orientation to the question.
- Read the question the second time, just to note and/or jot down the essential points or data.
- Read the question the third time. It is during this third time that you would start attempting to solve the problem. By this time, you would have seen the question "twice" before. This makes for a better understanding of the problem and all the requirements, givens, and unknowns.
- Read the question the fourth time. During this stage of reading, do a recapitulation of the problem, the boundary conditions, and a confirmation that you have answered the question as instructed.

One common example of the pitfall of not reading a question in its entirety is the famous 20-question test, in which the first instruction says to read every question before attempting to answer any of the 20 questions; and the last instruction says you don't have to answer any of the questions. Most students will impatiently start answering the questions as furiously fast as they can, because of the time constraint specified for the test. In the end, they never get to the end of the 20 questions within the limited time allotted for the test when, in fact, the test consists of only reading the 20 questions without having to do anything. Valuable time and stress are expended trying to beat the test time. This represents a big misapplication of effort and time. It takes a great amount of self-discipline to completely read a question before attempting to solve it. But if the upfront time is invested, it can save a lot of agony later on.

It is all about self-discipline.

Discipline of time management is essential for educational success.

Time is the basis for everything. Time, once lost, cannot be regained. My poem below presents his exhortation of the importance of time management.

"The Flight of Time
What is the speed and direction of Time?
Time flies; but it has no wings.
Time goes fast; but it has no speed.
Where has time gone? But it has no destination.
Time goes here and there; but it has no direction.
Time has no embodiment. It neither flies, walks, nor goes anywhere.
Yet, the passage of time is constant."
-     © 2006 by Adedeji Badiru

Time is of the essence of managing your academic tasks. Task management can be viewed as a three-legged stool with the following three main components:

- Time availability
- Resource allocation
- Quality of performance

When one leg is shorter than the others or non-existent the stool cannot be used for its expected purpose. Time is a limited non-recyclable commodity, as evidenced by the opening poem. Industry leaders send employees to time management training sessions and continuously preach the importance of completing tasks on time. However, the one area where time management is most crucial is often overlooked and undervalued, personal task management. Task management, by definition, is in itself time management via milestone tracking of important accomplishments and bottleneck identification. There are only 24 hours in a day and one of the goals for a student is how to most efficiently use those 24 hours. The tendency is for students to sacrifice the time portion of the academic pursuit and still expect the same level of performance. This thought process is flawed and ultimately leads to failure. If an academic semester task that normally takes twelve weeks for completion is condensed into four weeks, this would represent a time compression of more than 60 percent. If we were to take the task management stool and reduce one of the legs by 60 percent, the stool would topple over. This is the same result, in terms of performance, when activity compression occurs. An analysis of time constraints should be a part of the student's feasibility assessment of his or her study responsibilities. Task planning, personal organization, and task scheduling all have a timing component.

The precedence relationships among tasks fall into three major categories of technical precedence, procedural precedence, and imposed precedence. Technical precedence requirements reflect the technical relationships among activities. For example, in conventional construction, walls must be erected before the roof can be installed. Procedural precedence requirements, however, are determined by policies and procedures that may be arbitrary or subjective and may have no concrete justification. Imposed precedence requirements can be classified as resource-imposed, project status-imposed, or environment-imposed. For example, resource shortages may require that one task be completed before another can begin, or the current status of a project (e.g., percent completion) may determine that one activity be performed before another, or the physical environment of a project, such as weather changes or the effects of concurrent projects, may determine the precedence relationships of the activities in the project. An assessment of how tasks interrelate is a required element of not wasting time in task scheduling and management in the pursuit of sustainable education.

Chapter 5 References

1. Badiru, Adedeji B. (2019a), "Quality insights: Umbrella Theory for Innovation: A Systems Framework for Quality Engineering and Technology," *International Journal of Quality Engineering and Technology*, Vol. 7, No. 4, 2019, pp. 331-345.

2. Badiru, Adedeji B. (2019b), **Project Management: Systems, Principles, and Applications**, Second Edition, Taylor & Francis CRC Press, Boca Raton, FL, 2019.

3. Badiru, Adedeji B. (2020), **Innovation: A Systems Approach**, Taylor & Francis CRC Press, Boca Raton, FL, 2019.

4. Badiru, Adedeji B., Oye Ibidapo-Obe, and Babs J. Ayeni (2019), **Manufacturing and Enterprise: An Integrated Systems Approach**, Taylor & Francis/CRC Press, Boca Raton, FL, 2019.

Chapter Six

Summary of My Lessons from Saint Finbarr's College

As has been communicated throughout this book and my other publications, whether for home, work, and leisure, the influences of Saint Finbarr's shine through the pages. Since I give much credit to Finbarr's in a lot of things that I do, it is very important for me to share my story with readers across all genres. I hope through the examples presented in this book, other people can draw positive influences for their own personal and professional pursuits. If a reader can derive some inspiration from reading this book, then my job would have been done.

On the above note, I want to close with a short missive that I wrote in 2007 on the topic of social responsibility.

Wingman is Everyone's Social Responsibility

Social responsibility, along the line of what I learned at Saint Finbarr's College, is a favorite topic for me to talk and write about. What follows in a reprint of my newspaper article from November 2007 to celebrate the Thanksgiving season (Badiru, 2007). It is quoted as follows:

"This Wingman season reminds me of a social issue that has been on my mind for quite some time. The issue relates to the need for everyone to take on the social responsibility for everyone else, particularly the youth. The adage that "it takes a village to raise a child" has never been truer than in the present days of social uncertainties and inequities. Social stability and advancement of our society is everyone's responsibility. We cannot afford to look the other way whenever we notice something that is not right or something that does not bode well for the welfare of the entire society. Social issues that we fail to address now may magnify into incidents that could adversely touch everyone in the society, directly or indirectly. As individuals, we owe it to ourselves and our community to actively and directly participate in the resolution of societal ills. There is so much decadence evolving in society these days. Many of these deplorable social issues manifest themselves in the form of criminal activities brought on by feelings of frustration, disenfranchisement, isolation, depression, desperation, and hopelessness. When members of our community are noticed to be facing mental stress, financial discomfort, and despondency, it behooves all of us to jump in and offer helping hands. The extension of help can help preempt serious society problems later on. If we do not help, minor problems may become big felonious incidents that may come back to touch us in unimagined ways.

A community may think it is safe by cocooning itself within walls of its neighborhood. But the reality is that no one can be completely insulated from crimes that occur within the society. With freedom of movement and closing of geographical gaps, crime importation and exportation should be a big concern for every one of us. So, we should all share in the collective responsibility of helping to preempt the evolution of social decadence so that we don't have to deal with the results later on. It is obvious that prisons have become a huge drain on the society. Whether we want to accept it or not, we all pay for prisons. We pay in terms on loss of human capital, loss of loved ones, and impedance of economic growth. Wouldn't it have been cheaper to institute programs that would preempt criminal tendencies and, consequently, reduce the need for more prisons? For social ills, preemption is far better than incarceration. Programs that help to forestall crime are often cheap, subtle, and innocuous; such as offering social support to the less fortunate, providing a basis for optimism in youth, creating an atmosphere of belonging for everyone, offering encouragement, projecting empathy, and facilitating educational opportunities.

For youth, support, discipline, and comfort are as much a responsibility of the parents as they are of everyone in the society. We are not all too far removed from the possible adverse impacts of juvenile delinquency. Education is one sure way to advance the society and minimize criminal incidents. As an anecdotal example, there was once a socialite who was solicited to contribute to a program to improve educational programs in a neighboring community. He refused because he claimed that that other community should take care of their own problems. Many years later, one of the youths that could have benefited from the proposed educational program turned out to be a member of a gang of criminals who happened to operate in the socialite's neighborhood; and in the process murdered the socialite's loved ones. This is a good example of how a simple helping hand could have preempted later problems. What goes around comes around in unanticipated ways. Another case in point is the ongoing debate of whether the children of undocumented aliens should be accorded the same educational opportunities as everyone else. If you think this is not an issue of general concern for everyone, I urge you to think again. Think of the alternatives that those who are not educated might embrace later on in life. I invite all readers to consider these issues and their ramifications carefully. Although I have given talks about these social issues at various times, I believe the Skywrighter newspaper offers one more avenue to get the message out to a large Air Force Base audience. Have a nice season of Wingmaning and Thanksgiving."

The sense of this write-up is particularly relevant for the 2020 worldwide COVID-19 pandemic, in which we are summoned to take care of one another. Indeed, more social responsibility is needed during a pandemic that affects everyone of us, some in more adverse ways than others. To survive together is to watch out for one another. That's a great lesson I learned from Saint Finbarr's College.

In summary, Fidelitas!!!

Chapter Six Reference

1. Badiru, Adedeji, "Wingman is Everyone's Social Responsibility," *WPAFB SkyWrighter Newspaper*, November 30, 2007, Page 4A.

Appendix:

Educational, Aspirational, and Inspirational Quotes, Proverbs, and Dictums

Many guiding principles were learned at Saint Finbarr's College. Different students take away different lessons that serve them well for the rest of their careers, professions, and personal growth. Building life skills needed for success requires learning from direct experiences, observations, and inspirational social axioms. This appendix presents a miscellaneous collection of quotes, proverbs, and dictums that readers can adopt as useful takeaways for having read through this book.

"When curiosity is established, the urge to learn develops." – Deji Badiru

When Albert Einstein was still a lecturing professor, one of his students came to him and said:

"The questions of this year's exam are the same as last year's!"
"True," Einstein responded, "but this year all the answers are different."

"You cannot teach a man anything; you can only help him discover it in himself."
    - Galileo

"The urgent problems are seldom the important ones."
- President Dwight D. Eisenhower

"Life is like riding a bicycle. In order to keep your balance, you must keep moving."
- Albert Einstein

"You must learn from the mistakes of others. You can't possibly live long enough to make them all yourself."
- Sam Levenson (1911 - 1980)

"Common sense is seeing things as they are; and doing things as they ought to be." - Harriet Beecher Stowe

"Invest today in what will benefit you tomorrow, education." – Deji Badiru

Rita Mae Brown said,

"Lead me not into temptation; I can find the way myself."
- Rita Mae Brown, American writer, born 1944

"Success isn't permanent, and failure isn't fatal." - Mike Ditka

"There is no sunrise without sunset;
There is no life without death;
There is no success without failure."
- T. T. Rangarajan, Indian Guru

Success is often built on an experience of initial failure. When failure does happen, it should be not perceived as an absolute obstacle to success. For the sake of long-term education, a student must keep to the task of pursuing success no matter what the interim challenges might be. Don't quit!

"It has been my observation that most people get ahead during the time that others waste." - Henry Ford

"Don't judge each day by the harvest you reap but by the seeds that you plant."
- Robert Louis Stevenson

A bad beginning can make a good ending.
A student in debt is caught in a net.
A penny saved is a penny gained.
A stitch in time saves nine.
A wise man changes his mind sometimes; a fool never.
A word to the wise is enough.
Action speaks louder than words.
After a storm comes a calm.
All covet, all lose.
All bad things happen at night.
A pen is mightier than a sword.
All that glitters is not gold.
All work and no play makes Jack a dull boy.
All work and no fun makes Jane a dull gal.
All is well that ends well.
An empty bag will not stand upright.
An idle brain is the devil's workshop.
An ounce of discretion is worth a pound of wit.
An ounce of prevention is worth a pound of cure.
Appetite comes with eating.
Appetite for learning comes with reading.
As you make your bed, so you will lie on it.
As you sow, so you shall reap.
As you invest, so you shall collect.
Avoid evil and it will avoid you.
Be just before you are generous.
Be not the first to quarrel, nor the last to make it up.
Beggars cannot be choosers.
Better be alone than in bad company.
Books and friends should be few and good.
Brevity is the soul of wit.
By other's faults wise men correct their own.
By timely mending shall you save much spending.
Catch the bear before you sell his skin.
Catch who catch can.
Charity begins at home, but should not end there.
Cheapest can be dearest.

Curses are like chickens, they come home to roost.
Children are what you make of them.
Courtesy costs nothing.
Cut your coat according to your cloth.
Delays are dangerous.
Devil takes the hindmost.
Diligence is a great teacher.
Discretion is the better part of valor.
Distance lends enchantment to the view.
Do as you are told and you shall reap the reward.
Do not put all your eggs in one basket.
Do not count your chickens before they are hatched.
Do not spur a willing horse.
Early to bed, early to rise, makes a person healthy, wealthy, and wise.
Eat to live, but do not live to eat.
Employment brings enjoyment.
Empty vessels make the most noise.
Enough is better than too much.
Every cloud has a silver lining.
Every dog has his day.
Every little helps.
Every man must carry his own cross.
Every why has a wherefore.
Everyone can find fault, but few can do better.
Everyone thinks his own burden the heaviest.
Everything comes to those who wait.
Example is better than precept.
Experience teaches.
Extremes are dangerous.
Facts are stubborn.
Failure teaches success.
Fall not out with a friend for a trifle.
Fancy kills and fancy cures.
Fingers were made before forks.
Fire is a good servant, but a bad master.
Flattery brings friends, truth enemies.
Flies are easier caught with honey than with vinegar.
Follow the river and you will find the sea.

Fortune favors the brave.

Give and spend and God will send.

Good beginnings make good endings.

Good to begin well, better to end well.

Grass grows greener where you most need it dead.

Great haste makes great waste.

Great profits, great risks.

Great talkers are little doers.

Half a loaf is better than no bread at all.

Hasty climbers have sudden falls.

He knows most who speaks least.

He laughs best that laughs last.

He that comes first to the hill, may sit where he will.

He that goes a-borrowing, goes a –sorrowing.

He that knows nothing, doubts nothing.

He that will eat the kernel must crack the nut.

He who ceases to pray ceases to prosper.

He's no man who cannot say "No."

Home is home, though it never be homely.

Hope is the last thing that we lose.

If the cap fits, wear it.

If wishes were horses, beggars might ride.

If you wish for peace, prepare for war.

Ill got, ill spent.

In for a penny, in for a pound.

It is a long lane that has no turning.

It is always time to do good.

It is easier to get money that to keep it.

It is easier to pull down than to build.

It is never too late to mend.

It takes two to make a quarrel.

Jack of all trades and master of none.

Kind words are worth much, but cost little.

Kindle not a fire that you cannot put out.

Kindness begets kindness.

Least said, soonest mended.

Little strokes fell great oaks.

Live not to eat, but eat to live.

Loans and debts make worries and frets.

Lost time is never found.

Make hay while the sun shines.

Make short the miles, with talk and smiles.

Manners maketh man.

Many hands make light work.

Many straws may bind an elephant.

Marry in haste, repent at leisure.

Men make houses, women make homes.

Nearest is dearest.

Neither wise men nor fools can work without tools.

Never a rose without thorns.

Never cross the bridge before you come to it.

Never dam the bridge that you have crossed.

Never do things by halves.

Never look a gift horse in the mouth.

Never put off till tomorrow what may be done today.

Never too old to learn; never too late to turn.

Never trouble trouble until trouble troubles you.

New brooms sweep clean.

No gains without pains.

None so blind as those who will not see.

None so deaf as those who will not hear.

Nothing succeeds like success.

Oaks fall when reeds stand.

Of one ill come many.

Of two evils, choose the less.

Old birds are not caught with chaff.

On a long journey, even a straw is heavy.

One can live on little, but not on nothing.

One fool makes many.

One may sooner fall than rise.

One swallow does not make a summer.

One Today is worth two Tomorrows.

Other fish to fry.

Out of debt, out of danger.

Penny wise, pound foolish.

Practice thrift or else you'll drift.

Praise makes good men better and bad men worse.

Pride goes before a fall.

Procrastination is a thief of time.

Punctuality if the heart of success.

Punctuality if the soul of business.

Put not your trust in money; put your money in trust.

Put your own shoulder to the wheel.

Reckless youth makes rueful age.

Rumor is a great traveler.

Saying is one thing, doing is another.

Second thoughts are best.

Set not your loaf in till the oven is hot.

Show me a liar and I'll show you a thief.

Silence gives consent.

Six of one and half a dozen of the other.

Slow and steady wins the race.

Small beginnings make great endings.

Soft words break no bones.

Soft words win hard hearts.

Some men are wise and some are otherwise.

Sometimes the best gain is to lose.

Soon hot, soon cold.

Speak little but speak the truth.

Speak well of your friends, and of your enemy nothing.

Speaking without thinking is shooting without aim.

Speech is silver, silence is golden.

Spilled salt is never all gathered.

Still water runs deep.

That which is evil is soon learned.

That which proves too much proves nothing.

The best of friends must part.

The darkest hour is nearest the dawn.

The exception proves the rule.

The fountain is clearest at its source.

The game is not worth the candle.

The goat must browse where she is tied.

The heart sees farther than the head.

The less people think, the more they talk.

The morning sun never lasts the day.

The pot calls the kettle black.

The receiver is as bad as the thief.

The stone that lieth not in your way need not offend you.

The tongue always lashes the aching tooth.

The unexpected always happens.

The wise makes jests and the fool repeats them.

There are two sides to every question.

There could be no great ones if there were no little.

There is a "But" in everything.

There is no venom like that of the tongue.

There is a salve for every sore.

They who only seek for faults find nothing else.

Those who do nothing generally take to shouting.

Those who make the best use of their time have none to spare.

Time and tide wait for no man.

Time cures more than the doctor.

Time is the best counselor.

Tit for tat is fair play.

To err is human, to forgive is divine.

To forget a wrong is the best revenge.

To get more done, try and do less.

To know the disease is half the cure.

To make one hole to stop another.

To make two bites at one cherry.

To scare a bird is not the best way to catch it.

Too many cooks spoil the broth.

Too much of one thing is good for nothing.

Train a tree when it is young.

Tread on a worm and it will turn.

True love never grows old.

Trust, but not too much.

Two eyes see more than one.

Two is company, three is none.

Two hungry squirrels never quarrel.

Two wrongs do not make a right.

Undertake no more than you can perform.

Uneasy lies the head that wears the crown.

Union is strength.
Vice is its own punishment, virtue its own reward.
Walls have ears.
Wash your dirty linen at home.
Waste makes want.
Waste not want not.
We can live without our friends, but not without our neighbors.
Well begun is half done.
What belongs to everyone belongs to nobody.
What can't be cured must be endured.
What cost nothing is worth nothing.
What is learned in the cradle lasts to the crypt.
What's done can't be undone.
What is worth doing at all is worth doing well.
What man has done, man can do.
What the eye does not admire, the heart does not desire.
What the eyes don't see, the heart does not grieve for.
What the heart thinketh, the tongue speaketh.
When a man is going downhill, everyone will give him a push.
When in Rome, do as the Romans do.
When money is taken, freedom is forsaken.
When poverty comes in at the door, love flies out of the window.
When the cat is away, mice will play.
When the wine is in, the wit is out.
When two friends have a common purse, one sings and the other weeps.
When wits meet, sparks fly out.
Where ignorance is bliss, it is folly to be wise.
Where there is nothing to lose, there is nothing to fear.
While the grass grows the horse starves.
Who chatters to you will charter of you.
Who gossips to you will gossip of you.
Who judges others is only condemning himself.
Who knows most says least.
Willful waste makes woeful want.
Wine and wenches wreck men's wallets.
You cannot get blood out of a stone.
You cannot shoe a running horse.
You never know till you have tried.

Young men think old men fools; old men know young men to be so.
Youth and age will never agree.
Youth lives on hope, old age on remembrance.
Zeal without knowledge is a runaway horse.

Printed in the United States
By Bookmasters